LIVING WITH A STOMA

Dr Craig A. White is a chartered clinical psychologist with Consulting and Clinical Psychology Services (CCPS) in Ayrshire, Scotland. CCPS provides specialist psychological services to Ayrshire and Arran Community Health Care NHS Trust, North Ayrshire and Arran NHS Trust, South Ayrshire Hospitals NHS Trust and other organizations.

Dr White graduated with a first-class honours degree in psychology from the University of Glasgow, and then completed his doctorate in clinical psychology at the University of Manchester. He trained as a clinical psychologist on the North West Regional Health Authority rotational training scheme. His work within the NHS in Scotland involves clinical psychology as applied to the physical and mental health of adults.

Overcoming Common Problems Series

For a full list of titles please contact
Sheldon Press, Marylebone Road, London NW1 4DU

Overcoming Common Problems Series

Overcoming Common Problems Series

Overcoming Common Problems

Living with a Stoma

A practical guide to coping with colostomy, ileostomy or urostomy

Dr Craig A. White

sheldon PRESS

First published in Great Britain in 1997 by
Sheldon Press, SPCK, Marylebone Road, London NW1 4DU

British Library Cataloguing-in-Publication Data
A catalogue record for this book is available from the British Library

ISBN 0–85969–754–1

Photoset by Deltatype Limited, Birkenhead, Merseyside
Printed in Great Britain by
Biddles Ltd, Guildford and Kings Lynn

Contents

Acknowledgements

This book is dedicated to my wife Gwen in acknowledgement of her unfailing support for my work. It is also dedicated to my parents for their support and encouragement. My work on the psychological aspects of stoma care was inspired by Lynne Park, whose adjustment to life with a stoma and all that it has involved has been an illustration of the resilience of the human spirit.

I would also like to acknowledge all the stoma patients and stoma-care nurses I have met since I became interested in this area for their time and insights. I am grateful to Nicola Hamilton and Margaret Wagner for their patience and for providing secretarial support while I have been writing this book. Thank you to Andrew and Ann McPhail, and to colleagues who have shown an interest and encouraged me in my writing (especially Zena Wight).

Thank you to Sister Agnes Walls, clinical nurse specialist in stoma care, who commented on drafts of some chapters from the manuscript; to Jane Collier, senior dietician, who provided some information on dietary aspects of stoma care; and to Dr James Russell, consultant radiologist, who provided information and advice on radiological investigations.

To Gwen

1

Introduction

Approximately 52,000 people in the United Kingdom have a stoma. Around 15,000 new stomas are formed by surgeons in the UK each year. This book is concerned with the practical and emotional aspects of living with particular types of stomas called colostomies, ileostomies and urostomies. It does not cover the issues which relate to stomas such as gastrostomies or tracheostomies, and it does not provide information on stoma care for children.

If you do not already know what a stoma is then a brief and general explanation at this stage in the book might be helpful. A stoma is an opening which is created by a surgeon on the abdomen to allow waste-material (urine or faeces) to be expelled. A stoma is usually formed when the normal body systems for expelling waste-material are not functioning, due to an accident or a disease. The differences between colostomies, ileostomies and urostomies will be explained later in the book. You may already have a stoma and will therefore know that this involves a major change in the way your body works. If you do not have a stoma, or are about to have one formed, then I'm sure you can imagine that changing the way your body gets rid of waste-material is a major issue. This book is about the changes involved following stoma surgery, how to cope with these and how to get back to a normal life.

Many of the leaflets about adjustment to stoma surgery are extremely positive, presenting what I have heard some patients refer to as a 'jolly hockey-sticks' approach. Some leaflets show pictures of stoma patients playing tennis or sitting with all their family around them smiling. I am not suggesting that these pictures do not represent what is achieved by most stoma patients after their surgery. However, I believe that there should be more explicit acknowledgements that life with a stoma is not always easy to start with, that you are not unusual if you have problems or worries, and that any problems which crop up can usually be dealt with in a straightforward way. I hope that by reading this book you will find out about some of the possible problems, and that you can either prevent them from happening in the first place, or identify them early and develop coping strategies or ways of resolving the problems.

Stoma operations are usually life-saving operations. They are

1

almost always performed because there is no alternative. Medical staff recommend a stoma operation if a disease or physical problem is going to worsen without the operation. The fact that stoma operations are life-saving can make it easier for some people to get used to the stoma. However, I know some people who have had a stoma operation and, despite the knowledge that they would be dead without the stoma, they still find it difficult to live with. In other words, just because it saved your life does not necessarily make it easier to live with. Indeed, just because it saved your life does not mean that you have to like it. Life with a stoma can be difficult – even if it has saved your life. This book aims to help you lessen the potential problems of life with a stoma, and to really appreciate and enjoy the new life which stoma operations provide.

Approximately three years ago I realized that very little had been written by psychologists on adjustment to stoma surgery – and thus I decided to begin some psychologically-based research in this area. This is how my interest in adjustment to stoma surgery developed, and was the source of the initial idea for this book. In it I have tried to combine the 'common wisdom' from within stoma care with aspects of my work as a clinical psychologist, in order to provide practical information on stoma care as well as some unique ideas of my own about dealing with life with a stoma. Research into the psychology of living with a stoma shows that most people who have had the operation experience a certain amount of worry and concern as they adjust to life with a stoma. For most people this is part of a normal adjustment process following a major illness, major surgery and the experience of a change in the way their body looks and works. But other people who have stoma surgery – approximately 25 per cent of all those who have a stoma operation – experience more serious psychological symptoms after the surgery. People who have experienced psychological problems before stoma surgery are more likely to experience psychological problems after their stoma is formed. If this applies to you, then you should tell your doctor or nurse about this so that extra support can be provided. This book has been written for both groups of people – those who have minor difficulties which are part of normal adjustment and those who have more severe and incapacitating problems.

This book is primarily for the person who has had a stoma operation – though it is also for anyone who wants to find out more about what a stoma is and how it can affect quality of life. It will be useful if you or someone you know is to have a stoma operation, or if you are involved in looking after someone with a stoma. It aims to provide information on the practical and emotional aspects of coping with life after stoma surgery. It is not meant to be a substitute for the skilled advice and post-operative care which is provided by doctors, stoma-care nurses, surgeons and other healthcare professionals. I hope that it will reinforce and complement the advice and help given by these professionals. Not all healthcare professionals are knowledgeable about stoma care, as they may only occasionally come into contact with someone with a stoma. Most GPs will only have a couple of stoma patients within their practice, and may not be able to advise you on all aspects of stoma care.

As a clinical psychologist I am especially interested in promoting the best possible degree of psychological adjustment following stoma operations. This book has therefore been written with psychological adjustment in mind – to provide the kind of information and advice which doctors, surgeons and nurses may not give, and to do so in a way which can be of practical use to someone who is getting used to life with a stoma. Research has suggested that satisfaction with information is vital in helping people come to terms with surgery: I hope that this book will include all the information you could possibly need to get used to life with a stoma. In addition to providing general information on life after stoma surgery, I have tried to highlight problems which may need more than advice from a book. Certain physical or psychological problems require expert professional help. Unfortunately a large proportion of stoma patients with psychological problems do not receive professional help, as their nurses and surgeons do not notice that these problems are there. I hope that this book might be of some help if you have been suffering in silence, and that you might receive the right kinds of support and help as a result of what you read in it. If you are in any doubt at all about whether or not to speak to a nurse or doctor about a problem, then do not hesitate to contact them for advice.

What is in this book?

Like many other operations a stoma operation has wide-ranging effects on many different aspects of a person's life, and is carried out to cure or help alleviate the symptoms of particular diseases. You need to know about the disease and its symptoms, and why a stoma operation is being suggested in preference to another type of operation. Unlike any other operations, having a stoma involves having a stoma-care appliance ('bag' or 'pouch') and learning how to manage a stoma-care routine. So certain aspects of getting used to life with a stoma are common to recovering from any form of surgery – but there are many aspects which are unique to this type of operation.

Chapter 2 gives an overview of the anatomy and function of the human digestive and urinary systems – it is usually diseases in these bodily systems which are treated by a stoma operation. You need to understand how these body-systems work if you are to understand why a stoma is a helpful treatment, and how the surgeon creates a stoma. Chapter 3 outlines details of the different types of stomas covered in this book and how stomas are created. Chapter 4 provides detailed explanations of the various medical tests which might be carried out before and after the stoma operation, along with suggestions on getting the information you want about your disease, symptoms and treatment. Details on hospital staff whom you may encounter when in hospital are also given in this chapter. Life with a stoma means life with a stoma-care appliance – Chapter 5 includes all you need to know about stoma-care appliances and how to get used to them without major problems. This chapter also includes some helpful charts for you to complete to monitor your confidence in changing the appliance, to keep a note of how you get on with different appliances. There is also a 'troubleshooting guide' for appliance problems.

Thoughts about the stoma can contribute to problem-feelings, and Chapter 6 looks at how these feelings and thoughts can become negatively biased. This chapter includes some questions to help you to develop a thinking style which is less negatively biased about the stoma. The common emotional reactions to stoma surgery are explained in Chapter 7, along with some simple techniques to deal with them. The main focus of this chapter is on identifying the problem-thoughts underlying anxiety and depression, and there are details on how to change these problem-thoughts to help you feel better.

The next two chapters are focused on the effect which stoma operations can have on relationships. Chapter 8 deals with the effect of stoma surgery on relationships with other people in general, and on social interactions. The impact of stoma surgery on intimate relationships and sexual functioning is covered in Chapter 9, along with details on the human sexual response and common sexual problems. Chapter 10 covers some important aspects of enjoying life with a stoma – the various issues relating to travel, diet, work, sleep and sport are provided for those who need advice on these aspects of adjustment. You will find useful addresses and information on further reading at the end of the book.

Since I became interested in the psychological aspects of stoma care I have received some letters from patients who have developed problems in adjusting to their life with a stoma. I don't wish to discourage anyone from writing to me about how they have coped, the problems they have had (or are having), or how they have found this book useful. However, there are limits to the help that can be offered at a distance. If you are looking for individual help, my advice is always to go and discuss this with your GP first of all. You may wish to show your nurse or doctor some of the information and coping strategies outlined in the book. He or she might then be able to help you work through these as you apply them to your own problems. They will also be able to put you in touch with a specialist in stoma care or a specialist in psychological problems.

Summary

- Having a stoma operation involves a major change to the way in which the human body deals with waste-materials.
- This book includes all that you need to know about getting used to life with a stoma.
- Most people who have a stoma operation have some worries or concerns after surgery – these range from reactions which are part of the normal adjustment process to those which are part of more serious psychological problems requiring treatment.
- This book is not meant to be a substitute for the professional advice given to stoma patients by doctors, nurses and other health professionals. It aims to provide you with accurate information and to help you prevent, identify and cope with stoma-related concerns as well as you possibly can.

2

The digestive and urinary systems

Stomas are not often talked about. Because of this many people go through life without ever having heard of what they are. Sometimes we get ideas based on what we have heard from other people or what we have read in magazines. To understand what happens when a stoma is formed we need first to have some idea about how the digestive system and/or the urinary system works. This is because a stoma operation is usually the result of a problem with the digestive or urinary system. This chapter describes how both of these important bodily systems work, and then outlines some information on the common diseases which can affect each system. Chapter 3 then gives information on the various different stoma operations.

The digestive system

The way in which we digest our food seems so automatic – we don't need to think about it after we have swallowed. However, a lot happens in our bodies after we have swallowed our food. The main job of the digestive system is to break down (digest) our food into simpler parts so that the important nutrients which our bodies need can be taken into (absorbed into) the bloodstream. These nutrients are absorbed as the food makes its way through our digestive system. After the nutrients have been absorbed into our blood they can then be carried around the body to the parts of the body that need them most. Each part of the body takes what it needs for its own growth and repair. The digestive system also provides us with a way of getting rid of the waste-products which remain after our bodies have used all the nutrients that they need. The main parts of the digestive system are outlined in Figure 1.

After we have put food into our mouths it needs to be broken down before it can pass to the next stage in the digestive process. We begin to break the food down by chewing it. Saliva, produced by the salivary glands, mixes with the chewed-up food to break down the food even more. Once the food has been chewed and mixed up with the saliva, it is then ready to pass down the oesophagus. The oesophagus is a flattened muscular tube which is about 30–40 centimetres in length. The food travels down the oesophagus into the stomach. When the

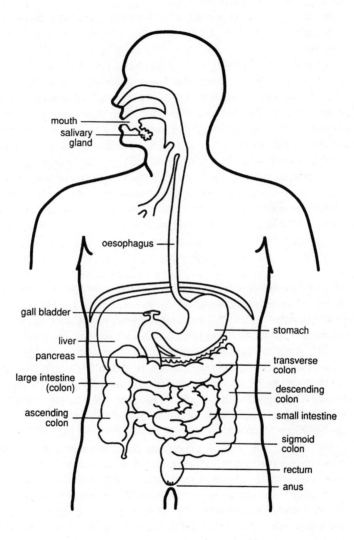

Figure 1 The digestive system

food reaches the stomach, the next stage of the digestive process – called gastric digestion – can begin.

The stomach is a like a hollow bag in which the food is mixed with digestive juices and churned up (a bit like a liquidizer). The stomach does this mixing by making slow churning movements. The juices from the stomach (called gastric juices) and the food are thoroughly mixed together until the mixture has a gruel-like consistency. This gruel-like fluid is called chyme. It can take anywhere between one and six hours for the food you put in your mouth to be changed into chyme, depending on what you have eaten. A simple meal, such as a cup of tea with bread and butter, is digested in the stomach in around one hour – whereas a meal which contains eggs, milk or meat might take three hours. A heavy dinner, which includes soup, meat and/or fruit, can take up to seven hours to digest fully in the stomach and become chyme.

The chyme then passes into the small intestine, where digestion can continue. The small intestine is a long, twisting maze of tube about six metres in length. The chyme is converted, by fluids from other parts of the body, into a yellow, creamy fluid called chyle. The chyle moves along the small intestine, and as it goes, all the nutrients from the food are absorbed through the walls of the intestine. Most of the goodness from food-materials is absorbed in the small intestine. The leftovers now have to be dealt with by the other parts of the digestive system.

The remains of the food keep passing along the digestive system, moving from the small intestine to the large intestine. The large intestine is another long tube, which is about 1.5 metres long, and wider than the small intestine. This is where the final stages of digestion happen. The main job of the large intestine (or colon) is to absorb water and other important chemicals into our bodies from the food. When the colon has done this, waste-material (called faeces) is all that is left. The faeces are moved down the colon by sweeping muscular contractions called peristalsis. You may have noticed that the urge to pass faeces comes on after eating food. This is because eating can trigger these muscular contractions. These cause waste to move further down the digestive system. The faeces pass down to the rectum, which acts like a storage tank for the waste-material – and for any food which could not be digested as it travelled through the digestive system. When the rectum is full, we get the desire to pass the waste-material. When it is convenient, we get rid of the waste by the relaxation of the internal and external muscles of the rectum. The abdominal and pelvic-floor muscles are contracted and the waste-material is then expelled through the anus – the opening at the end of the rectum. This is the final stage of the digestive process.

The urinary system

The main parts of the urinary system are shown in Figure 2. The kidneys are complex organs which filter out the waste-products from our blood. After they have done this, they flush out waste-material through two narrow tubes called ureters. The ureters feed into the bladder – a hollow organ in the lower part of the abdomen which acts as a storage area for urine. Urine is the liquid waste which is made by the kidneys when they have cleaned the blood supply. When the bladder is almost full of urine, a message is sent upwards to the brain telling it that the bladder is nearly full. When it is appropriate to do so, relaxing of the sphincter muscle causes the urine to flow out of the urethra – a similar action as when we relax the muscles above the anus to let the faeces out.

Problems with the digestive system

It is essential to understand the basics of the digestive and urinary systems if you are to understand what a stoma is and why it is sometimes necessary. Now we have seen how these systems work, we shall look at some of the main diseases which can cause problems with these systems. Sometimes these diseases are treated by an operation in which a stoma is formed. Understanding the main diseases will make it easier to understand why a stoma operation is sometimes done to help with a particular disease.

These digestive-system diseases are the most common ones to be treated by a stoma operation. Some of the symptoms mentioned can be caused by other, less serious, conditions.

Ulcerative colitis

Ulcerative colitis is a disease in which the lining of the large intestine (including the rectum) becomes inflamed and ulcerated – these ulcers can weep and bleed. Ulcerative colitis can occur at any age, though people aged between 20 and 40 are most commonly affected. Five thousand people develop this disease in the UK every year. Its main symptoms are diarrhoea mixed with blood, mucus and/or pus, stomach-ache, loss of appetite, sickness, weight-loss, a frequent need

9

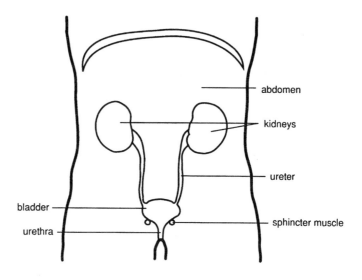

Figure 2 The urinary system

to empty the bowels and pain at the anus. This disease tends to come and go. Sufferers have periods between flare-ups when they feel completely well – these are called periods of remission. The treatment for most patients with ulcerative colitis is drugs. Sometimes an operation is needed because the drugs are not working, or because the ulcerative colitis has worsened very quickly. People with ulcerative colitis have a higher chance of getting bowel or rectal cancer – they may have a stoma operation because of this higher risk.

Crohn's disease

Crohn's disease is also an inflammatory bowel disease. Just like ulcerative colitis it can occur at any age. Unlike ulcerative colitis, Crohn's disease can occur anywhere in the digestive system, from mouth to anus. With this disease, part of the digestive system becomes inflamed and develops ulcers. The most commonly affected area of the digestive system is the last part of the small intestine (terminal ileum)

10

and part of the colon or rectum. The symptoms of Crohn's disease are bleeding from the anus, colicky abdominal pain after meals, weight-loss, diarrhoea with mucus and/or pus, fever, nausea, vomiting, lethargy and loss of appetite. Most people who have Crohn's disease need to have an operation.

Familial polyposis coli (Gardner's Syndrome)

Familial polyposis coli is a condition where the large intestine develops polyps (pronounced 'pollups') which are at risk of becoming cancerous. This disease is inherited. Every child of a parent with this disease stands a 50:50 chance of developing it themselves. Children of parents who have this condition need to have regular check-ups when they reach their teenage years to see if they have developed any polyps.

Diverticular disease

Diverticular disease is common after the age of 40. It affects about one third of people over the age of 60. Someone with diverticular disease may have few symptoms – they may not know that they have it. A lack of fibre in the diet can be a contributory factor to the development of this disease. This lack of fibre results in small, hard bowel-movements which are difficult to move along the bowel. This then produces high pressure in the bowel which causes pouches to form. These pouches develop through the bowel wall and are called diverticulae. Faeces can become trapped in these pouches and can cause irritation. If this happens, inflammation, pain, altered bowel habits, abdominal disten-sion and bleeding can develop. A high-fibre diet may be recommen-ded, or sometimes an operation is suggested.

Colorectal cancer (sometimes called bowel cancer or rectal cancer)

Colorectal cancer is a disease where (malignant) cancer cells are found in the large intestine and/or rectum. It is one of the UK's most commonly occurring cancers. This disease usually comes on gradu-ally, and symptoms may not occur until the later stages of the disease. The symptoms of this disease are the passing of mucus or slime from the anus, distension of the abdomen, abdominal pain, a change in bowel habits, bleeding from the anus or a sense of fullness in the back passage. The main treatment for bowel and rectal cancer is the removal of the part which is affected – this may or may not mean that a stoma operation is needed.

Cancer of the anus

Cancer of the anus is an uncommon cancer. Symptoms of this cancer can include bleeding from the rectum, pain in the area around the anus, a lump near the anus and itchiness or a discharge of fluid from the anus.

Problems with the urinary system

Cancer of the bladder

Cancer of the bladder is a disease where (malignant) cancer cells are found in the bladder. Blood in the urine (called haematuria), frequent urination, a burning sensation when passing water, and a feeling of needing to urinate although nothing comes out – all are common symptoms of bladder cancer. In the UK, bladder cancer accounts for about 7 per cent of all male cancers and 2.5 per cent of all cancers in women.

Problems with the digestive or urinary systems can also result from accidents in which damage has occurred to a part of the body (inside or outside) which is needed for the digestive or urinary system to work properly. Radiotherapy treatment for cancer can also cause damage to important organs, and this damage can cause problems. Problems with the urinary system can also be caused by diseases of the nervous system such as multiple sclerosis.

Summary

This chapter has covered important information on how our digestive and urinary systems work. It has also provided some details of the diseases which can cause problems with these important systems. Sometimes these diseases are treated by arranging for the person to have an operation in which a stoma is formed.

- The digestive system is responsible for taking the food we eat, making sure that our bodies get all the important nutrients they need and then getting rid of the waste-material.
- The main parts of the digestive system are the oesophagus, stomach, small intestine, large intestine, rectum and anus.

- The urinary system deals with the liquid waste from our bodies after our kidneys have filtered out waste-materials from our blood supply.
- The main parts of the urinary system are the kidneys, ureters, bladder and urethra.
- The main diseases which affect the digestive system and which may need a stoma operation are ulcerative colitis, Crohn's disease, diverticular disease, colorectal cancer and polyps.
- The main disease which affects the urinary system and which may need a stoma operation is cancer of the bladder.

The next chapter will explain some more about the different types of stomas, and how they are created.

3

Stomas

This chapter describes the most common types of stomas and outlines what happens when a surgeon carries out a stoma operation. It is crucial that you understand why a stoma operation is recommended, and that you are able to talk to doctors and nurses without becoming confused. The main stomas covered here are a colostomy, an ileostomy and a urostomy.

The terms used for stoma operations can be split up to help us understand them. The second part of each word ('-stomy') means to form a new opening or outlet. The word 'colostomy' is made up of 'colon' and '-ostomy' – 'colon' being the large intestine – the whole word thus meaning 'to form a new outlet for the large intestine'. The word 'ileostomy' is made up of 'ileum' and '-stomy', and describes the formation of a new opening for the small intestine. The word 'urostomy' is made up of 'ur-' and '-stomy' and refers to the creation of a new outlet for urine. One common factor in all stoma operations is that a new opening or outlet is created by the surgeon. The other common factor is that a part of the inside of your body is brought out on to its surface to make the new opening. Stomas are moist and red in colour (like the inside of your mouth). They have no nerve-endings and are not sensitive to being touched. Stomas may make a sort of gurgling noise sometimes when they are producing waste-material or when gas escapes.

What is a colostomy?

Colostomy is the name given to the opening which is made during an operation, when the large intestine (the colon) is brought to the surface of the abdomen so that waste-material comes out there instead of travelling down to the rectum (as described in Chapter 2). A colostomy is the most common type of stoma. It is usually formed after treatment for colorectal cancer or cancer of the anus. To make a colostomy, the surgeon cuts a hole in the patient's tummy and sews a piece of bowel to the skin surface. This piece of bowel forms the stoma. Instead of the large intestine travelling all the way down to the rectum, it has been diverted out on to the surface of the body. If the rectum is not removed

14

then the surgeon may also bring the cut end of the rectum to the surface of the body. This small opening is called a mucous fistula. The colostomy is usually situated to the left of and just below the level of the tummy-button.

A colostomy operation is also sometimes carried out when there has been an injury to the rectum which cannot be repaired. When the rectum has been damaged during a person's illness, the surgeon sometimes removes the anus and the lower part of the rectum. When the rectum, anus and part of the colon are removed in this way, and a colostomy is formed, the operation is called an abdominoperineal resection.

After an operation of this type people may experience the sensation that they are going to have a 'normal' bowel movement from their rectum. This sensation is known as 'phantom rectum', and can be distressing for the person who experiences this if they are not prepared for it. They feel as if they are going to have to pass a motion, but they know that their rectum has been removed. You may have heard of people who lose limbs or fingers yet who experience a sensation as if the limb or finger were still there. This 'phantom limb' phenomenon occurs because the nerves which supplied the limb are still in place, even though the limb has gone. The brain still thinks that the limb is there. This is what happens with phantom rectum – the nerves to the rectum are still intact, even thought the surgeon has removed the rectum itself. The brain 'thinks' that the rectum should get ready to pass the motion. Phantom rectum is a normal sensation, and usually passes as time goes on and as the brain gets used to the fact that waste is expelled from the stoma and not from the rectum.

Temporary colostomy

A colostomy may only be created as a temporary arrangement when a diseased part of the bowel has been removed, so that the remaining parts of the bowel can have time to heal. It is sometimes formed temporarily when the surgeon wants to observe how another part of the digestive system is working. A temporary colostomy might also be formed when an injury to the anus or rectum needs time to heal. With a temporary colostomy the waste-material is diverted away from a part of the digestive system (e.g. the rectum or anus) to the abdomen until it is safe for it to pass along its usual route again. This is a bit like a road diversion where cars are diverted to another route until the old road is repaired.

The rectum is left in place when the colostomy is only a temporary arrangement. This means that the large intestine, which is diverted to the abdomen, can be joined up to the rectum again at a later date.

Loop colostomy

Sometimes a 'loop colostomy' is made. This is almost always a temporary arrangement. A loop colostomy is when a loop of bowel is brought to the surface of the skin and opened up. It is supported by a rod. Only one of the two openings actively produces waste-material. The two openings can be joined again at a later date.

Other types of colostomy

You may remember from Chapter 2 that by the time the food reaches the large intestine it has been transformed into chyme, then into chyle, and that, in the large intestine, water and chemicals are absorbed. The consistency of the waste-material which comes out of the colostomy depends on which part of the large intestine the surgeon has diverted on to the abdomen. If the surgeon diverts a piece of the large intestine which is further along and nearer the rectum, then the waste which comes out of the stoma is harder than if he/she had diverted a piece of intestine at the beginning of the large intestine. This is because more water has been absorbed by the time the waste has reached the parts of the large intestine nearer the rectum.

The decision about which part of the large intestine to bring out on to the abdomen depends on the position of the disease in the digestive system. Figure 1 (page 7) shows the different parts of the colon – the ascending colon, the transverse colon, the descending colon and the sigmoid colon. You may sometimes hear the terms 'transverse colostomy' or 'sigmoid colostomy'. These terms define which part of the large intestine has been brought out on to the abdominal surface. A sigmoid colostomy, for example, is a colostomy in which the sigmoid section of the large intestine has been redirected to form a new outlet on the abdominal surface.

What is an ileostomy?

Ileostomy is the name given to an opening which is made during an operation in which the small intestine is brought to the surface of the abdomen so that waste-material comes out there, instead of travelling on within the digestive system to the large intestine. An ileostomy usually comes out on the bottom right-hand side of your abdomen. The waste-material which comes from this type of stoma is much more watery (a bit like porridge) than the waste which comes from a colostomy. The waste from an ileostomy contains digestive enzymes which are harmful to the skin. Because of this an ileostomy always sticks out more than a colostomy does – this helps to keep these chemicals away from the skin as much as possible. An ileostomy is usually situated to the right, and just below the level of, the tummy-button.

When all of the colon, rectum and anal canal are removed and an ileostomy is formed this operation is called a pan proctocolectomy with ileostomy. This is always performed as a permanent arrangement. Sometimes the surgeon performs an operation called a total colectomy with ileostomy. This means that the colon is removed but the rectum stays in place. The rectum is either just left or it can be diverted to the abdominal skin-surface to form a mucous fistula. This can sometimes be done if the surgeon is thinking of doing more surgery in the future. He/she needs to keep the rectum in place because of the possibility of more surgery.

Earlier in this chapter we saw what a loop colostomy was. It is also possible to make a 'loop ileostomy'. This is where a loop of small intestine is brought to the skin-surface and fixed so that one end forms a spout. The other end is an opening which leads to the large intestine. This is usually done as a temporary arrangement – the ends can be rejoined at a later stage.

Alternatives to ileostomy

Surgeons are always developing new techniques and there are variations on the operations mentioned above which I have not mentioned. This book does not aim to provide you with details on all possible surgical procedures which may be carried out. A surgeon is always the best source of information on these techniques, and will be able to tell you if this is relevant to your particular situation. However, I have decided to include some information on two increasingly popular alternatives to ileostomy surgery which mean that patients are not obliged to wear an appliance at all times. These alternative surgical procedures are called the Kock pouch and the ileo-anal pouch.

The Kock pouch

A Kock pouch is made by creating a pouch and a small valve from the small intestine. The patient inserts a catheter through the valve to drain off the contents. This usually happens four to five times each day. This operation is not suitable for everyone.

The ileo-anal pouch

Surgery to create an ileo-anal pouch is not appropriate for diseases such as Crohn's disease. An ileo-anal pouch is a specially created pouch, which holds waste-material and which is joined to the anus. This means that waste-material is expelled from the anus as normal. This happens more frequently though (four to six times a day and once at night), and the waste-material is very loose.

An ileo-anal pouch is created in stages. The first stage involves the removal of the colon and the formation of a temporary ileostomy. A pouch is then made from part of the small intestine and this is then attached to the anus. The final stage is when the temporary ileostomy is reversed and the waste-material can then pass through the pouch. The muscles around the anus need to be strong for this operation to work. Special assessments and exercises to strengthen these muscles may be recommended. It can take longer to get used to an ileo-anal pouch than it does to get used to an ileostomy. If you think that this may be a possibility for you, then discuss it with your doctor.

What is a urostomy?

Urostomy is the name given to an opening which is made during an operation in which urine is diverted to the surface of the abdomen so that it can be collected there, instead of being stored in the bladder and then passed away through the urethra. Urostomies are usually carried out when the bladder has to be removed (cystectomy). In this operation a piece of the small intestine is removed and brought out on to the surface of the person's body. A urostomy is usually situated to the right of, and just below, the level of the tummy-button. The tubes which carry urine (the ureters) are sewn on to the end of the piece of small intestine, allowing the urine to flow out of the stoma. A urostomy is sometimes called an ileal conduit or urinary diversion stoma.

Two stomas

Sometimes people have two stomas created. Some people already have one stoma and then need to have another one because they develop a different disease. Other people have to have two stomas made at the same time (because of the nature or spread of their illness). These are created in the same way as has been described for one stoma. Living with two stomas can be particularly difficult – though many of the issues are the same as those which occur when someone has one stoma – issues which this book aims to cover.

Deciding the position of the stoma

The decision on where the stoma should come out of your abdomen is a very important one – and one in which you are involved (unless it's an emergency operation). One important consideration is that you need to be able to see the stoma, because this is helpful when it comes to looking after it. It is also important to check that the position is suitable for you whether you are sitting, standing or lying. The stoma-care nurse should be involved in helping you choose a site for the stoma. The nurse checks that possible sites for the stoma will not interfere with clothing (e.g. trousers) – and also takes many other things into account, such as the presence of scars, the position of your tummy-button, creases in the groin, the waistline, fatty bulges, the place where the surgeon will make the cuts and any areas affected by skin problems.

When you have decided with the nurse on a position for the stoma, this will be marked with a special marker-pen. At this stage some people start to worry that they might not be able to wear the clothes that they used to. I once saw a patient who was upset because she thought she would have to discard all her clothes. There may be individual items of clothing that you feel less comfortable wearing. But there's no reason why certain garments (e.g. tight jeans) can't be worn if you wish. Having a stoma does not mean having to buy a completely new set of clothes.

Sometimes it is necessary to have a second operation at a later date to move the stoma slightly or tidy it up in some way. This is referred to as 'refashioning' the stoma. Further operations can sometimes be necessary if you have problems – such as a prolapse (your stoma sticks out more) or a retraction (the stoma falls in) – which need attention.

Summary

This chapter has explained the main types of stoma which can be created. Some of the factors which are important in siting the stoma have been outlined. You have now read about the way the digestive system works, some of the problems which can arise, and the main stoma operations which are carried out to treat these diseases. To show yourself that you understand what a colostomy, ileostomy or urostomy is you might want to try explaining this to a family member or friend.

- Colostomy is the name given to an opening which is made during an operation in which the large intestine is brought to the surface of the abdomen. There are different versions of this operation (e.g. abdominoperineal resection or loop colostomy).
- Ileostomy is the name given to an opening which is made during an operation in which the small intestine is brought to the surface of the abdomen. There are different versions of this operation (e.g. pan proctocolectomy or loop ileostomy).
- There are now some alternatives to ileostomy surgery which avoid the need to wear a stoma appliance – the Kock pouch and ileo-anal pouch are examples of this. Surgeons are able to advise you on these operations.
- Urostomy is the name given to an opening which is made during an operation in which urine is diverted to the surface of the abdomen. This is done by joining the ureters on to a piece of small intestine.
- The important decision on exactly which part of the abdomen to site the stoma is made before the operation, by a specially trained nurse or doctor who makes a decision based on you as an individual.

The next chapter will cover some of the main issues which will be important for you to know about before you have your stoma operation.

4

Hospitals

This chapter provides information on various aspects of your contact with hospitals – having tests done, the people whom you might meet there, and the operation itself. There can be a lot to cope with at this time, and having some information on what to expect is likely to be helpful. So much happens to you when you are at the hospital that it can be very difficult to remember it all. Having the information you want, and being satisfied with it, is an important part of beginning life with a stoma.

One of the most important factors which determines how well someone adjusts psychologically to an operation is whether they are satisfied with the information they receive. You will have your own ideas about the information you would like to have before the operation. Make a list below of the questions you would like to have answered before the operation: this way, you will not forget what you want to know, and there is a better chance of getting all your questions answered.

My information needs

Before the operation

For example: How long will I be in hospital before my operation? Will any tests be carried out? What are they?

Question:

Answer:

....

Question:

Answer:

....

Question:

Answer:

....

Question:

Answer:

....

Question:

Answer:

....

During the operation

For example: How many people will be at the operation? What will the surgeon do if it looks worse than he thought?

Question:

Answer:

....

Question:

Answer:

....

Question:

Answer:

....

Question:

Answer:

....

After the operation

For example: Will the stoma start working straight away? How will I know if the operation has worked or not? Will my sexual functions be affected?

Question:

Answer:

....

Question:

Answer:

....

Question:

Answer:

....

Question:

Answer:

....

Now that you have thought about what you would like to know, you can begin to tick off each question as it is answered. This book may help answer some of your questions. The doctors, nurses and other hospital staff are also important people from whom to get information. Once you have listed all your questions, you can tell your nurse or doctor about the list and ask to work through it with them. You might be worried that the nurse or doctor will be too busy, or that you are being a nuisance. But remember that answering a patient's questions and providing information is part of their job – if you are worried about them being too busy, you can ask them to set aside time to come to discuss your questions later. You might be embarrassed about asking certain questions, or unsure how to go about this. There are no easy answers on how to overcome embarrassment. You might want to confide in a nurse or other member of staff who will help you to overcome your embarrassment, or you might want to ask if a friend or family member could be with you when you ask your questions.

Before you go for your operation you can tick off the information you have been able to get. This way you can see if there are still things which you would like to know about. It is really important that you get the information you want, that you get it at the right time and that you remember it. You will notice that some nurses and doctors make notes when they are asking you questions, to help them remember what you tell them. Similarly, to remember what they tell you, you should also write down their answers to your questions – in the spaces provided above, if you wish. You will thus have a reminder of what was said, which can be referred to later on. This can be really useful when you need to explain various details of your situation to others, such as relatives or friends. It can also help if you want to read it over again yourself.

Medical tests

There are certain tests which doctors carry out to help them decide what is wrong, and which treatment is the best one for you. You may already have had some of these tests – or you might have them in the future. The main medical tests which people have before or after an operation to make a stoma are outlined below.

Barium enema

A barium enema allows the X-ray examination of the large intestine. A thick, liquidy substance (barium liquid) is fed into the large intestine by means of a tube which is inserted through the anus. Some air is also blown into the bowel to help obtain more detailed X-rays. Barium is a substance which shows up on an X-ray, enabling the doctor to spot any possible problems – such as inflammation or ulcers.

This test is not painful, though you may feel a little uncomfortable for a short time. The test lasts for no longer than 30 minutes from beginning to end. You are given laxatives to take on the day of your appointment for the barium enema. If you have a morning appointment, you are asked to have no breakfast. For afternoon appointments you are allowed to have a light breakfast before 8 a.m., but you must have nothing to eat or drink after this. In some cases barium enema tests are arranged after the stoma operation, so that the surgeon can check the bowel. The barium liquid is then inserted through the stoma.

CT scan

A CT or computerized tomography scan is a specialized form of X-ray examination which provides pictures of internal organs not accessible to normal X-ray machines. A CT scan is carried out when the doctor wants to get pictures of certain internal parts of your body. You lie on a flat surface while the scanner rotates around you, producing images of the inside of your body. When you have a CT scan of the abdomen or pelvis, you are given a small quantity of liquid to drink about one hour before you are scanned. You should expect to be at the hospital department for a CT scan for between 30 minutes and two hours.

Intravenous pyelogram (IVP) or intravenous urogram (IVU)

An IVP or IVU is an X-ray of the kidneys and bladder. You are given a special dye containing iodine, usually by injecting it into a vein in your arm. The dye shows up the various parts of the urinary system on the X-rays, revealing whether there are any problems, and if so, where exactly they are.

Some people say that they feel hot and flushed when the dye is injected. But there is no pain and there are no after-effects involved with this test. You need to follow a special diet for three days before your test appointment. This is called a low-residue diet and includes foods such as lean meat, boiled potatoes, well-cooked root vegetables, tea, fruit juice, plain biscuits and strained soup. You are also required to take laxatives before the appointment. For a morning appointment you should not eat anything on that day, and for an afternoon appointment you should have nothing to eat or drink after a light breakfast. The test is usually finished within one hour.

Ultrasound

Ultrasound uses radio waves to look inside the body without using X-rays. Ultrasound is used to look at developing babies in the womb – and is also used in other areas of healthcare to examine other parts of the body. A little gel is applied to your skin, and a small scanner is moved over the surface of your body to take pictures of what is happening inside. The same eating restrictions apply to this test as to a barium enema (see above). You are required to drink a pint of diluting juice or water before the ultrasound, and you must not empty your bladder before the test. The bladder needs to be full for this test.

Sigmoidoscopy

This test is done when the doctor wants to be able to see the anus, rectum and sigmoid colon (see Chapter 2). A long, flexible tube with a light on the end – called a sigmoidoscope – is inserted through the anus and rectum. The doctor can see inside your body by looking through a mini-telescope at the end of the tube. Using this technique it is also possible to take a piece of the bowel away to look at it carefully under a microscope (this is called a biopsy). This can help hospital staff to decide on what is wrong. This test takes a maximum of 20–30 minutes and may involve your being given a mild sedative tablet.

Colonoscopy

Sometimes doctors want to see all of the large intestine (or colon). A long, flexible viewing tube – called a colonoscope – is inserted into the colon through the anus and rectum. People who have this test are often given a tablet or an injection to make them sleepy. It is possible to feel the tube moving inside you when you have this test. As with a sigmoidoscopy, this may feel a little uncomfortable for a short time. This test is perfectly safe, and lasts for a maximum of 30 minutes from beginning to end.

Cystoscopy

This test is similar to a sigmoidoscopy, but instead the flexible tube (cystoscope) is inserted through the urethra (see Chapter 2) and then into the bladder. This means that the doctor can see if there is anything wrong in the bladder. A small piece of tissue can be removed from the bladder to be examined under a microscope.

General information

For most of these medical tests you will be asked to take all your clothing off and change into a gown. Most tests do not require a general anaesthetic – but if this is required, you will be told about it; you may still have the test done as a day-patient. Perhaps there are other tests which have not been mentioned and which you do not know about – ask your nurse or doctor to explain what is involved.

If you have to go for a medical test you may be feeling very nervous. Some people understandably get very uptight about going for a test, and may dread it from the minute they are told it is needed. You can do some things to reduce your nervousness about going for a medical test.

- Having some factual information on the test can be helpful. When we do not have information, we tend to 'fill in the blanks' by predicting that negative things will happen and that we won't be able to cope. Getting accurate information helps us to challenge these ideas. Hospital staff might be able to give you an information leaflet if you ask them. You might also want to find out the answers to the following questions before you have a test: What does it involve? Why is it being done? How long will it take? Will it be painful? What might the results show? When will I find out the results? It can help to find out if anyone else who you know has had the test done – they might be able to tell you about what happened and how they coped with it. But research has shown that there are some people who prefer not to have information – if this is what you prefer, then it may be the best option for you. The important thing is that, whatever information you ask for (however small), you get answers which satisfy you.
- Another thing which can be helpful in coping with medical tests is to think up things to say to yourself during the test. Examples of this would be: 'This is OK, I can cope with this and take it one step at a time'; 'This is only for a minute, it is to find out what is wrong with me'; or, 'I can do this, no problem; I know what is happening, this is to help me'.
- You might also want to keep your mind occupied while the test is going on. There are various ways in which you can do this. One way is to imagine a delightful scene, and to focus on it in detail (the sights, sounds, smells and colours) during the test. Some people picture a pleasant holiday they have enjoyed, or imagine themselves in a really relaxing situation, or at an enjoyable family event. Another way of distracting yourself is to play mental games: count backwards from 100 in sevens (e.g., 100, 93, 86, etc.); or think of as many words as possible beginning with 'S' within one minute; or try to come up with the name of a town for every letter of the alphabet. These mental distractions help to block out thoughts which might cause distress during the test. This distraction technique may also be helpful at other times when you want a quick way of coping with anxious or worrying thoughts.

Who's who at the hospital

In the course of your contact with the hospital, you will meet many different health professionals. It can sometimes be confusing when you have to meet so many different people with different jobs and sometimes obscure titles. The following list covers the staff whom you are most likely to meet when you are in hospital. There may be other health professionals who are involved in your care – if you do not know who they are or what they do, then ask them to tell you.

House officer

House officers are doctors who have completed their medical training and are gaining further training and experience (usually for 12 months) before becoming fully recognized medical practitioners. House officers usually spend six months working in surgery. You are likely to meet a house officer when they are arranging for tests and assessments soon after you go into hospital. They may carry out some of these tests (e.g. blood tests) themselves.

Senior house officer (SHO)

An SHO is a fully qualified medical doctor who is gaining more experience, or who has chosen to work in a specific area of medicine or surgery – in other words, you might meet an SHO in surgery or an SHO in general medicine. Some SHOs may be training to become GPs. SHOs are involved in arranging tests, assessing symptoms and recommending treatments.

Registrar or senior registrar

Registrars are doctors who have completed specialist training and taken further exams in one particular area of medicine. They have overall responsibility for some of the patients they see. They will eventually become consultants. It may be a registrar or senior registrar who performs the stoma operation.

Consultant

A consultant is a senior doctor who has responsibility for a particular area of medical care within a hospital – such as surgery (consultant surgeon); urology (consultant urologist); medicine (consultant physician). A consultant is usually directly involved in planning your treatment with you – for example, in deciding what tests to order, and what treatments to recommend.

28

Oncologist

An oncologist is a doctor who specializes in the diagnosis and treatment of cancers.

Urologist

A urologist is a doctor who specializes in the diagnosis and treatment of problems associated with the urinary system.

Stoma-care nurse

Stoma-care nurses are specialist nurses who have been trained in the care of people before and after surgery to create a stoma. They have special expertise in all aspects of stoma care – including teaching patients to look after their stoma; giving information and advice; supporting patients; helping with stoma-care routines and advising on problems such as leakage. The stoma-care nurse is the main person who helps before and after the stoma operation.

Occupational therapist (OT)

OTs are the healthcare professionals with special expertise in advising on daily living activities, such as cooking and dressing. They might help someone who is having these practical problems by advising on new ways of dealing with the activities, or by providing aids to help make the activities easier. You might come across an OT if you have this type of problem, in addition to having a stoma formed.

Physiotherapist

Physiotherapists are skilled in helping patients to become active as soon as possible after an operation. Difficulty with movement can be common after a stoma operation – and this inactivity can mean an increased risk of infections and other problems. The physiotherapist usually visits before an operation to explain what will happen, and may also teach you some simple breathing and movement exercises.

Clinical psychologist

Clinical psychologists are specialists in the way people feel, think and behave. They have expertise in the psychological aspects of physical and mental health, and are trained to carry out psychological assessments and treat people to enable them to overcome problems with their feelings, thoughts and/or behaviour. Stoma patients might see a clinical psychologist if they have developed problems with anxiety, depression or sexual problems after surgery.

Dietician

Dieticians have special expertise in the science of nutrition, and they use their knowledge to promote nutritional well-being, to treat disease and to prevent nutrition-related problems. Stoma patients usually receive advice on diet from their stoma-care nurse – but a dietician may be involved if specific nutritional problems develop. Dieticians want to assess your own diet-history and to gather information on your weight and any changes in this.

The operation

Before you go for the operation to make a stoma, you will have to make sure that your bowel is as clear of food and waste-material as possible. This is called bowel preparation. This can be done in different ways – you will have to stop eating the day before the operation, and you might be given an enema or some laxative tablets. An enema is a medicine which is inserted up your anus. The enema makes you want to go to empty the contents of your bowel. Its purpose is to make the bowel as clean as possible for the operation. This means that the bowel is easier to see when tests are being done – and, more importantly, it means that there is less chance of an infection developing in the bowel after the operation.

It is important that you are as satisfied as you possibly can be with the information you get about the stoma operation before you undergo it. This may include, before the operation, seeing photographs of what the stoma will look like – or even meeting someone who has had a stoma operation. Every person is different – there can be no hard-and-fast rule about what is the best thing to do. But if you have not yet had your operation and you think you might want to see a stoma or meet someone who has one, then talk this over with the people who are looking after you. The stoma-care nurse will help you reach a decision about what seems to be the best option for you. If you do decide to meet someone who has had a stoma operation, please remember that this is just one person – if you have a concern or a problem which they did not mention, then this does not mean that you need to be especially worried. Everyone is different.

People who have had their stoma for many years can be very

positive about their life with a stoma. Some patients, awaiting their stoma operation, undoubtedly find this very helpful. However, it can also cause problems for others, who imagine that they will never be so positive. Remember that getting used to life with a stoma is a gradual process. Even if you experience a few hiccups along the way, these can usually be sorted out and you can be helped back on track again. There are people who want to do all they can to help you with whatever problem might develop. Sometimes people who have had their stomas for some years, and who get involved with visiting patients, tend to focus only on the positives. I am sure that if you ask them to tell you honestly that they will tell you about their worries too.

After the operation you will probably have tubes and drips going into your body. Some of the tubes are to make sure that fluids and drugs can get into your body; others help get rid of fluids and waste-material from your body. You will probably have a tube up your nose, called a nasogastric tube. This tube travels down to your oesophagus and into your stomach; it will probably stay in until your body starts to recover from the operation and work as it is supposed to. You will probably take a couple of days before looking at your stoma. The stoma will be much much bigger at first than it will be in a few weeks. It will get smaller as each day passes, usually settling at about two or three centimetres in diameter.

If you have had a colostomy or ileostomy you will notice that there is no waste-material produced for a few days. This is normal. You will also find that there is a foul smell when the bag is changed for the first time. Just as the stoma is much bigger at first, so is the smell worse in the early days. This is because your bowel has not been working for some days. There has been a build-up of bacteria inside, and it is this that makes it smell so bad. Unlike a colostomy or an ileostomy, a urostomy starts to work almost immediately after the operation.

Summary

- Being satisfied with the advance information which you get about both the operation and the stoma is an important part of beginning life with a stoma.
- You might have to have medical tests such as barium enema, CT scan, intravenous pyelogram, sigmoidoscopy or cystoscopy. Understanding what will happen during these tests can make them easier to cope with.

- There are a number of practical ways whereby you can reduce anxiety before the tests and make the tests themselves easier to cope with.
- The many different hospital staff can be confusing – don't be afraid to ask them what their jobs are and why they are seeing you!
- Before the stoma operation, some people want to look at a picture of a stoma or talk to someone who has had their stoma operation – think about whether you would find this helpful.
- A stoma is much bigger and much smellier just after the operation than it will be in the days and weeks afterwards.

The stoma-care nurse is there to help you learn how to look after the stoma, and will make sure that you can do this before you go home. Learning how to look after the stoma means that you need to learn about stoma-care appliances – 'bags' or 'pouches'. The next chapter outlines the different types of appliances, and helps you think about your stoma-care routine and how to incorporate this into your everyday life. It is important that you are confident about looking after your stoma before you go home. There is a diary in the next chapter to help you to keep track of your confidence in looking after the stoma.

5

The stoma-care routine

'Before I left hospital, most of the self-pity that I'd felt had been erased by learning from the experience of others. I was introduced by the stoma nurse to different appliances and taught how to change the bag and clean the area. By the time I was discharged I was using a one-piece disposable bag, feeling positive and was supplied with my purpose-filled "box of tricks"' (Male colostomy patient, aged 63).

When you have a stoma operation, not only do you need to get used to life with a stoma but you also need to get used to life with stoma-care appliances. People have different preferences about the name they give to their stoma-care appliance – some people call it a 'bag', whereas others prefer to call it a 'pouch'. I will refer to it as an 'appliance' in this chapter. The stoma appliance is a specially manufactured device to collect the waste-material produced from the stoma. After you have had a stoma operation, you need to learn what is involved with your new routine for getting rid of waste. This means learning a new set of skills and becoming familiar with a new set of words to describe the various parts of the stoma appliance and the tasks associated with changing it. Eventually this new routine becomes a habit – just like the old habits of disposing of waste, before the stoma operation.

Stoma-care appliances

Stoma-care appliances come in either one or two pieces.

The **one-piece appliance** has a bag to collect waste-material (this has a hole in it which fits neatly around the stoma) and an outer ring. This outer ring (called a flange) is adhesive and sticks securely to your skin to keep the appliance in place. You can buy appliances with holes already cut to the size of your stoma (most manufacturers provide guides to measure stoma sizes). Alternatively, you can buy appliances which do not have holes cut in them and then cut the hole in the flange to fit your stoma exactly. All of a one-piece appliance – the bag and the outer ring – is disposed of when the bag is full of waste-material. The whole thing (bag and outer ring) is then replaced with a completely new appliance. There is a separate section on the disposal of stoma-care appliances later in this chapter.

The **two-piece appliance** has a base-plate which fits around the stoma. The base-plate is fitted with adhesive material to make it stick to your skin. The second part of the two-piece appliance is the bag which fixes on to the base-plate. Unlike a one-piece appliance, it is only the bag which is disposed of – so that the plate does not need to be removed each time you change the bag: it can stay in place and a new bag can be clipped on when you have disposed of the old one.

Stoma-care appliances can be drainable or closed.

A **drainable stoma-care appliance** can be opened at one end so that the contents can be emptied or drained away. Drainable appliances are usually used by people who have an ileostomy. They may also sometimes be used straight after a colostomy operation, when the waste-material is very liquid and it is easier to drain the contents. You may remember from Chapter 3 that the waste-material from an ileostomy is loose in consistency – this means that a drainable appliance makes emptying easier.

Closed stoma-care appliances do not have an opening at the end. They are therefore more suited to use when the waste-material is more solid (as with most colostomies).

Stoma-care appliances can be either transparent or opaque. The transparent (see-through) appliance can be very helpful when you want to be able to see the stoma and the waste-material. This may be important in the early stages following your operation: it will help you to see the stoma while you are getting used to all that is involved with the stoma-care routine. It may be helpful for you or your doctors to see the waste-material. Doctors might observe the colour and/or consistency to check on your progress. Getting the appliance in the correct position over the stoma can be easier with a transparent appliance. When you do not need or want to see the stoma or the waste-material, then there are opaque appliances which have a pattern or a tint on them.

There are various combinations of stoma-care appliance available: one-piece closed opaque; two-piece closed opaque; one-piece drainable transparent, etc. Now that you know what each of these terms means, you can appreciate what makes each of these appliances different. Learning about stoma-care appliances is a bit like having to learn to use a new language.

Urostomy appliances are slightly different from the appliances used most commonly for colostomies and ileostomies. Because urine is produced much more frequently than faecal waste, the appliances which are used for urostomies are designed to be worn for longer periods. Urostomy appliances have a drainage tap and valve to prevent the urine from travelling back up near the stoma when the patient is lying down. This is very important, because it reduces the chances of infection. The rest of an appliance for a urostomy is similar to those used for colostomies and ileostomies.

Most people with a urostomy will have to use a night drainage system when they are asleep. This means that the urine is being collected in a larger pouch overnight. The pouch is fixed to a stand. If you have a urostomy and are worried that the pouch might leak, then the stand for the night drainage-bag can be placed in a basin – so if there is a leak, it goes into the bowl and not onto the carpet.

There have been many advances since the days of the first stoma-care appliances. I have read many stories of people who had to use things like thick, black rubber bags for collecting waste from a stoma – and even having to improvise using a baked-bean tin. Most colostomy and ileostomy bags nowadays are fitted with a special carbon filter which deodorizes (takes the smell away from) the gases which can come from the stoma. Appliances are made of materials which are odour-proof and which do not make too much noise when you are moving around. The flange is made of a special material which is designed not to irritate your skin.

Changing the appliance

Learning to change the stoma-care appliance is an important part of adjusting to life with a stoma. Initially you may think that it will never become 'routine', or that you will never have confidence, or get used to what is involved. This may or may not be true – you will find out for yourself as time goes on. Women patients might find it helpful to think back to when they first learned to deal with the hygiene routine associated with menstruation. Did you have doubts that you would be able to get used to it? Were you super-confident at inserting a tampon or using a sanitary towel on the first few occasions? You probably did have doubts and were not super-confident to start with. And you almost certainly became more confident as time went on. Changing the stoma appliance is the same – you probably have some doubts to start with, but with time it will become easier as your confidence increases.

Male patients might compare the situation with things that they weren't confident about to begin with – for example, the doubts about cutting yourself the first time you used a razor, or the process of learning to ride a bicycle or change the tyre on a car. If you think about how you were the first time you did these things and compare then with now, you will notice that you have fewer doubts and more confidence as time has gone on.

You will probably develop your own particular routine for changing the stoma appliance. However, there are some basic stages which you must go through to change the appliance safely. One of the most important things to note is that most appliances *do not* go down the lavatory, as this would cause a serious blockage.

Some people are not sure when to change their appliance. There are no hard-and-fast rules about this and with time you will probably find out what works best for you. However, it is generally not a good idea to wait until the appliance is almost overflowing with waste-material before you change it. You will get into a routine eventually.

There are certain items which you need every time you change the appliance. Some people find it helpful to collect these and put them into a little box or bag to keep them together. Some people have two sets – one which stays at home and the other to take out as a portable stoma-care tool-set.

Each time you change the appliance, you will need the following items:

- new appliance;
- measuring guide;
- kitchen-roll or swabs;
- paper bag, plastic bag or newspaper;
- small pair of scissors;
- small mirror.

Once you have all these items, you are ready to begin. The following steps are the main ones which you will go through each time you change the appliance:

1 Locate and lay out all the items that you will need for changing the appliance.
2 Take off the old appliance.
3 Empty the contents of the old appliance into the toilet. If you have a closed appliance, then this is done by cutting it with a pair of

scissors. A drainable appliance can be drained into the toilet. Rinse the appliance by holding it under the flush of the toilet. Sometimes you can avoid splashing from the toilet bowl by placing a couple of sheets of toilet-paper or kitchen-roll on the water before you empty the appliance contents.

4 Wrap the old appliance in newspaper or put it into a plastic bag.

5 Wipe around your stoma with a piece of kitchen-roll or a swab and then wash around the stoma with warm water.

6 Pat the area around the stoma dry with a piece of kitchen-roll or swabs.

7 If you use any accessories (e.g. creams) then they should be used at this stage.

8 Put on the new appliance. If it is a two piece appliance start with the base-plate first of all. With urostomy bags: remember to make sure that the tap is closed. With ileostomy bags: remember to make sure the clip is tightened.

9 The old appliance (wrapped and placed in a bag) can now be placed in the dustbin. Some councils have a service to collect clinical waste and may arrange this for you if you wish.

You may find it helpful to use a safety-pin when you are changing the appliance, to pin your clothing up out of the way.

Looking after the stoma: self-care checklist

There are certain things that you should be able to do to look after your stoma before you leave hospital. It may also be a good idea to make sure that there is someone else who can do these things to look after your stoma – just in case something happens which prevents you from doing it yourself. Some people with a stoma find it reassuring to know that there is someone else who is able to change the appliance if they are unable to do so.

I suggest that you rate your confidence in four stages:

1 after you have tried the main steps in the stoma-care routine for the first couple of times, when you are about to go home;

2 one week after you go home;

3 a month after you go home;

4 three months after going home.

This can be a good way of helping you to see your increasing confidence in looking after the stoma.

You can rate your confidence by using a 0–10 scale for each of the tasks. A score of 0 would mean that you were not confident at all at that task, whereas a score of 10 would mean that you could not be more confident in your ability to carry out that task. The scores between 0 and 10 indicate different degrees of confidence.

Rating 1

Date: ....   at hospital/at home (*circle one*)

Removing the appliance from my skin (0–10) ....

Emptying the appliance (0–10) ....

Washing and drying stoma and skin (0–10) ....

Measuring the stoma (0–10) ....

Putting the appliance on (0–10) ....

Getting rid of the used appliance (0–10) ....

Rating 2

Date: ....   at hospital/at home (*circle one*)

Removing the appliance from my skin (0–10) ....

Emptying the appliance (0–10) ....

Washing and drying stoma and skin (0–10) ....

Measuring the stoma (0–10) ....

Putting the appliance on (0–10) ....

Getting rid of the used appliance (0–10) ....

Rating 3

Date: ....   at hospital/at home (*circle one*)

Removing the appliance from my skin (0–10) ....

Emptying the appliance (0–10) ....

Washing and drying stoma and skin (0–10) ....

Measuring the stoma (0–10) ....

Putting the appliance on (0–10) ....

Getting rid of the used appliance (0–10) ....

Rating 4

Date: ....   at hospital/at home (*circle one*)

Removing the appliance from my skin   ....
(0–10)
Emptying the appliance (0–10)   ....
Washing and drying stoma and skin (0–10)   ....
Measuring the stoma (0–10)   ....
Putting the appliance on (0–10)   ....
Getting rid of the used appliance (0–10)   ....

When you have rated this on four different occasions, check to see if your confidence ratings are staying the same, getting worse or improving. If they are not getting any better you may want to speak to your stoma-care nurse about this. It may be that there is a problem which is making you less confident about the stoma-care routine. The nurse will be able to help with this. If you notice that your confidence is increasing, then you might want to think about how this relates to your previous doubts that you would never learn to do the various tasks. This will be a helpful exercise should you ever try to read into the future – as you did when you first had the stoma.

New developments in appliance disposal

Disposing of a stoma-care appliance is not the easiest thing in the world. It involves having to spend longer in the bathroom than you did before your stoma operation, having closer contact with your own bodily waste-material, and having to carry all sorts of extra items into the bathroom. Recent developments in stoma care aim to make appliance disposal more of a 'normal' experience. Developments in scientific technology have meant that some used appliances can now be flushed straight down the toilet – the bags are strong enough to contain the waste-material when they are being worn (even during swimming), but they gradually disintegrate into biodegradable products when they are flushed down the toilet. At the time of writing these disposable bags are only available to people with a colostomy – but scientists are working on developing similar appliances for use with ileostomies. Information on appliance manufacturers can be found in the 'Useful information' section at the end of the book.

Getting supplies

Before you leave hospital you should have been given the details of the appliances which you have been using. You will thus know what to get when you need fresh supplies. A space has been left for you to write this information in the table below. If you have not been given this information, then you should ask the ward sister or your doctor about it:

Appliance make:	....
Appliance type:	....
Appliance manufacturer:	....
Code:	....
Number in pack:	....
Monthly quantity:	....

Stoma-care appliances have to be issued on prescription – in the same way that some drugs have to be issued. You may already know about getting what is called 'a repeat prescription' from your GP – repeat prescriptions are the easiest way of getting stoma-care appliances. If you have a stoma then you are eligible for an exemption from *all* NHS prescription charges. To be granted this exemption you need to complete a P11 form, which is available from your GP, stoma-care nurse or from any post office. Exemption certificates are usually issued for a period of five years.

In other words, to get your stoma-care appliances you need to get a prescription, go to the pharmacist and collect the items – in the same way you would collect a prescription for tablets or other medicines. At the moment the prescription for stoma-care appliances has to be issued by a doctor (though it is usually the stoma-care nurse who advises the doctor about what you need). Most GPs are advised by clinical nurse specialists in stoma care about what appliances should be prescribed. You may have heard about developments to allow nurses to write prescriptions for certain items, such as skin-dressings (this is experimental in some areas of the UK at the time of writing) – and it may be that, in future years, stoma-care nurses will issue prescriptions for stoma-care appliances.

Testing different appliances

In the early stages of your life with a stoma you may try various different appliances – either because you experience problems with some, or because you become aware of new appliances which you want to try. Different appliances suit different people. Use the chart below to note down any appliances that you try, your ratings for them and any other comments which you may have about them.

These charts enable you to keep a note of the dates when you are trying out the appliance – as well as its make and manufacturer. You can then rate how comfortable it is to wear that particular appliance, how confident you feel wearing it and how easy you find the changing and disposal routine. For each of these, use a 0–10 rating: if you were rating an appliance for comfort, then a score of 0 would mean not at all comfortable, while 10 would mean the most comfortable appliance you could imagine.

Trial period: From: ....   To: ....
Appliance manufacturer: ....
Appliance make: ....
Comfort rating   (0–10):   ....
Confidence rating   (0–10):   ....
Ease of change and disposal rating(0–10):   ....

Comments: ....
....
....
....

Trial period: From: ....   To: ....
Appliance manufacturer: ....
Appliance make: ....
Comfort rating   (0–10):   ....
Confidence rating   (0–10):   ....
Ease of change and disposal rating(0–10):   ....

Comments: ....
....
....
....

Trial period: From: ....   To: ....
Appliance manufacturer: ....
Appliance make: ....
Comfort rating   (0–10):   ....

Confidence rating   (0–10): ....

Ease of change and disposal rating(0–10): ....

Comments: ....

....

....

....

Trial period: From: ....   To: ....

Appliance manufacturer: ....

Appliance make: ....

Comfort rating   (0–10): ....

Confidence rating   (0–10): ....

Ease of change and disposal rating(0–10): ....

Comments: ....

....

....

....

Rating each appliance you try can be a good way of deciding on which one is best for you – you can keep a note of your ratings and refer back to them when you want to compare your old appliance with any new ones that come along. If you had not rated appliances, or kept a note of how you got on, you might have forgotten. This would make it more difficult to compare new appliances that you try out.

Leaks

You may, at some stage, experience some leaks from the stoma appliance. This can be very difficult to cope with, causing embarrassment and anxiety about going out. Stoma-related physical problems, like leaks, have also been shown to be associated with psychological difficulties like anxiety and depression. If you keep having leaks, contact your stoma-care nurse or GP to have it checked. It may be that there is something they can do to stop the leakage. Below is a list of some common reasons why leaks may occur – you may be able to help stop your leaks by consulting this and making certain adjustments.

Leakage troubleshooting guide

Cause of leakage	*Solution*
Appliance not sticking to the skin properly.	Make sure that the skin around the stoma is very dry. When the appliance is stuck on, hold your hand over the stoma and appliance for 60 seconds to warm it and to ensure that you have the best seal possible.
Folds or creases in your skin are getting in the way.	You can get special pastes to fill in the cracks (a bit like Polyfilla for humans). This makes the surface flatter and it is easier to stick the appliance on. Speak to your stoma-care nurse if you need help or advice about this.
The skin around your stoma is irritated.	This can be difficult as you can get stuck in a vicious cycle (especially with an ileostomy) whereby you have a leak which irritates the skin – and this means the appliance then does not stick as well to your skin. The best solution for this is in trying to keep the skin around the stoma as healthy as possible.
Not emptying the appliance often enough.	Overfilling of the appliance can break the seal because of the weight of the waste-materials. Try to empty the appliance before it becomes too heavy. This stops it from pulling on the sticky seal.
The materials of the flange can be affected by high temperatures.	You could try changing the appliance more frequently in warm weather, and/or experiment with a change of flange material.

| Appliances not being stored properly or for too long. | Stoma-care appliances do not last forever. They should always be stored in a cool and dry place. You may want to find out from the manufacturer of the appliance how long they recommend it be kept for. |

There are sometimes alternatives to wearing a stoma-care appliance all of the time. People with a colostomy may be able to use a soft foam plug which fits into the stoma, so that there is no need to wear an appliance. They have to ensure that they wear an appliance at some point, to collect waste-material. It is also possible to use a technique called irrigation. This involves introducing flowing water into the bowel from the stoma to ensure that waste-material is expelled. Irrigation enables the person with a colostomy to have more control over their bowel movements. More information on plugs and irrigation can be obtained from your stoma-care nurse.

Summary

- Getting used to life with a stoma also involves getting used to stoma-care appliances – what they are and how to change them.
- Stoma-care appliances can be one-piece or two-piece, closed or drainable and transparent or opaque.
- Changing a stoma-care appliance can be difficult at first, but like anything new it becomes easier with practice. Your doubts will disappear and your confidence will increase.
- There are many different kinds of stoma-care appliance – trying different types and makes of appliance is often the only way to discover which one is the best for you.
- Leaks can occur sometimes. They are often associated with common problems which can be easily sorted out.
- Plug or irrigation techniques are alternatives for some patients who prefer these to wearing a colostomy appliance.

6

Thoughts about your stoma

The way we think about things is extremely important in determining how we feel, what we do and what physical reactions we have. Events or situations do not cause our feelings – rather, our feelings come from the thoughts we have about events or situations. Similarly, events don't cause our behaviour, but the thoughts we have about the events. This is important in trying to understand the different emotional, behavioural and physical reactions of people who have a stoma operation.

To see the importance of thoughts in our everyday lives, consider this example. You are sitting reading this book on getting used to life with a stoma:

1 You think: 'This book is really interesting and has some good ideas to help me.'
   How do you think you might feel if you thought this? (*circle one*)
   Depressed   Enthusiastic   Frustrated   Happy
   What do you think you might do if you thought this? (*circle one*)
   Take book back to shop   Stop reading   Keep reading it
2 You think: 'This book is boring – I have wasted my money and could have bought something else more useful.'
   How do you think you might feel if you thought this instead? (*circle one*)
   Depressed   Enthusiastic   Frustrated   Happy
   What do you think you might do if you thought this? (*circle one*)
   Take book back to shop   Stop reading   Keep reading it
3 You think: 'I don't understand any of this – I am so hopeless, nothing ever goes right for me.'
   How do you think you might feel if you thought this instead? (*circle one*)
   Depressed   Enthusiastic   Frustrated   Happy
   What do you think you might do if you thought this? (*circle one*)
   Take book back to shop   Stop reading   Keep reading it

You will notice that you had different feelings and different actions depending on your thoughts about the situation. The situation was exactly the same (sitting reading this book). But your thoughts were different each time – so your feelings and behaviours were also different. The situation did not change – but your thoughts were different in the very same situation.

In exactly the same way it is your thoughts about the stoma which determine your feelings and behaviour towards the stoma after the operation. Your thoughts about the stoma determine whether you feel anxious, contented or gloomy about it, and whether you behave similarly to the way you always did or whether you have developed new and different reactions, such as avoiding meeting new people.

There are some common themes in the thought-patterns of people who have had a stoma operation. I have carried out some research in this area and have listed below some of the thoughts commonly experienced by people who have had a stoma operation. To find out whether you have these thoughts, put a circle round 'agree' or 'disagree' beside each stoma-related thought. Try to answer each question as honestly as you can – this in itself may help you recognize some of the negative thought-patterns about your stoma.

1	My stoma rules my life.	*Agree*	*Disagree*
2	No one can tell that I have got a stoma.	*Agree*	*Disagree*
3	I am less confident in myself since I have had a stoma.	*Agree*	*Disagree*
4	No one understands what it is like to have a stoma.	*Agree*	*Disagree*
5	I smell because of my stoma.	*Agree*	*Disagree*
6	I can take part in the same activities as I used to despite, my stoma.	*Agree*	*Disagree*
7	I feel less of a real man/woman since my stoma operation.	*Agree*	*Disagree*
8	I feel that I am in control of my body following my stoma operation.	*Agree*	*Disagree*
9	My stoma might leak if I go out.	*Agree*	*Disagree*
10	I can be near to other people without worrying about my stoma.	*Agree*	*Disagree*

11	My stoma is repulsive.	*Agree*	*Disagree*
12	Other people can see my bag through my clothes.	*Agree*	*Disagree*
13	I am still a complete person despite my stoma.	*Agree*	*Disagree*

The rest of this chapter focuses on these common thought-patterns regarding a stoma. It shows you how to step back from them and begin to modify some of these negative stoma-related thoughts. This is important in helping you to overcome negative feelings, such as anxiety or depression about your stoma. Changing your thinking about the stoma is also important in changing your behaviour related to it. (The next chapter has detailed information on how to identify negative thought-patterns and problem-thoughts, and on how you can then begin to modify them to help you feel better.)

Altering negative thought-patterns

Once you have identified your negative thoughts about your stoma, you can begin to change them as the first step in feeling better in yourself and behaving differently. This can be very difficult. The following sections are based on your answers to the questionnaire above, and are designed to help you modify your thinking about having a stoma. Each section heading describes the thought-pattern, and beneath it are the statements and answers ('agree' or 'disagree') which show negative thought-patterns and which are the subject of that section.

'I'm not in control any more'

Question 1: My stoma rules my life.   *Agree*
Question 8: I feel that I am in control of my body following my stoma operation.   *Disagree*

If you believe that your stoma rules your life or that you are no longer in control of your body, you are likely to feel sad, gloomy or even depressed. Ask yourself: 'In what way does my stoma rule my life? Does it rule my life 24 hours a day, seven days a week – or is it just part of the time?' Is it helpful to use the word 'rules' – or is this a bit extreme? Would it be more helpful to say to yourself that the stoma only affects how you live your life, not that it rules your life?

47

If you think about it, most people have something or other which affects how they live their lives. Most of us have to take at least a number of different factors into account when planning our lives – and a stoma can be thought of as another factor that needs to be taken into account. If the stoma only affects your life for part of the week, then you can make a plan to work round this and to get on with your life at other times. One way of doing this is to keep a weekly diary of how your stoma influences your life, and then to use this information to plan your life around it. You do not have control over when your stoma is working – that is a fact. Does this mean that you are not in control of your body? Were you always in control of your body before the stoma operation? Did you ever have the experience of your stomach rumbling when you were with other people? Were you in control of your body then? You may not have control over when the stoma works, but you can develop control over what effect this will have on you. You don't have control over when you will get a headache, but you can learn to cope with this by developing some control – such as taking a tablet, relaxing or having a snooze. Does having less control mean that you have none whatsoever?

Thinking of control as something which is completely present or completely absent is not likely to be helpful. Would it help you to think in terms of having degrees of control? Some days, at certain times of the day, you may have 60 per cent control – whereas at other times you will have different amounts of control. The stoma can only rule your life, and take away your own control, if you let it.

'Everyone knows about my stoma'

Question 2: No one can tell I have got a stoma. *Disagree*
Question 10: I can be near to other people without worrying about my stoma. *Disagree*
Question 12: Other people can see my bag through my clothes. *Agree*

If you think that people can tell you have had a stoma operation, ask yourself how other people know about it. They may know because you have mentioned it to them, or because they have heard from someone else. If this is the case, then what is it about this that is a problem for you? You may be worried that they will be thinking negatively about you because of this. But if you heard that someone you knew had a stoma, would you think negatively of them? I suspect that you wouldn't. If you wouldn't think negatively about someone with a stoma, how likely is it that people will think negatively about you? Are the people you know really so different from you? You may be worried about a complete stranger knowing that you have had a stoma operation. If you are, then think carefully about how they could possibly know about it.

You might be worried that other people can tell that you have a stoma because they see a bulge in your tummy or hear an unexpected noise. Even if they do notice a slight bulge on your tummy (though this is unlikely unless someone is looking right at that one part of you for a long period of time), how do you know that they would think that it was a stoma? How many people know what a stoma is anyway? Most people who are troubled by this thought overestimate the degree to which other people are aware of the stoma. They also behave as if they can mind-read – as if they know what other people think about them. To show yourself how difficult it is to detect a stoma, try and pick out five people with a stoma the next time you have a day out. Remember that thousands of people have stomas – so if they are that obvious then you should be able to pick out a few. If you are unable to do this, perhaps it will help you to think again about how easy it is to identify someone with a stoma by just looking at them. One of my patients said that having a stoma was like having a ladder in her stocking – she knew it was there, but nobody else did.

'It's impossible for anyone to understand'

Question 4: No one understands what it is like to have a stoma.   *Agree*

Although you may sometimes think that no one understands, how can this be true? Many other people have had stoma operations – and even if they can't understand everything that you are experiencing, is it possible that they might understand most of what is happening to you? Perhaps to understand part of what you have been through is a start? Some people have had major operations – so they probably know something of what you have experienced. Others may know people who have stomas. Most people can piece together different parts of their life experience to try to understand what you are going through.

You may have been thinking that friends, family and the people you know don't understand what it is like to live with a stoma – that they don't have one, and it's therefore difficult for them really to know how it feels. But to understand something do you have to have experienced

49

it yourself? Is it possible never to have experienced something, yet still to understand some of what it might be like? Is it possible, for example, for you to understand what it might feel like to be blind? If you were to close your eyes then you might get some idea. In other words, even though you are not blind you can imagine and understand part of what it might be like not to see.

It is true that some people don't understand everything about your life with a stoma – but they may be able to imagine some of it, and understand part of your experience by drawing on their own experiences and those of other people. Is this good enough? If you don't understand something, does it help you when someone else explains it? If so, do you think that it might be easier for other people fully to understand your situation if you were to give them an explanation? You will never find that out unless you try to explain, and then ask them if it has helped them in any way to understand. In any case, do other people really need *fully* to understand?

'I'm smelly'

Question 5: I smell because of my stoma. *Agree*

Is it really true to say that it is *you* who smells because of the stoma? Is it not the waste-material that smells? There is a difference. You may think that other people can smell the urine or faeces produced by the stoma, and this thought may make you feel depressed or anxious. But remember that your nose is right above the stoma, so any smell is stronger to you than it is to other people who are further away (and whose noses are not directly above it). There may be a horrible smell when you have to empty the appliance in the bathroom – but is this really different from everyone else? The smell I produce in the bathroom, without a stoma, is sometimes quite revolting (as my family will tell you). Telling yourself that it is you who smells doesn't help you to feel good about yourself. Perhaps you would feel better if you could remind yourself that it is the waste-material that smells, not you. You might also remind yourself that all modern appliances are made of odour-proof materials.

'I can't do the things I used to'

Question 3: I am less confident in myself since I have had a stoma. *Agree*

Question 6: I can take part in the same activities as I used to despite my stoma. *Disagree*

50

Immediately after the operation there are certain things that you won't be able to do, usually as a result of your having had major surgery. Does the fact that you are not able to do them now mean that you will never be able to do them again? Has there ever been a time in your life when you have been unable to do something for a while, but later you could do it again? If this has happened before, is it possible that it could happen again? When you started it again, did you start from where you left off or did it take some time gradually to build up to where you were? Might it be the same with the stoma – that at first you can't do all the things you used to, but that as you recover you will be able to pick up some things, gradually working back to your old routine?

The key to dealing with this thought is to consider the things that you can still do, and to keep a note of the new things you can do on each new day – for example, you might notice that you can walk longer distances. Keeping a diary is a good way of noting your gradual progress. You could start this now: note down two things you do each day which are new activities, or activities you feel are easier than yesterday or the day before.

'I'm not a complete person any more'

Question 7: I feel less of a real man/woman since my stoma operation. *Agree*

Question 13: I am still a complete person despite my stoma. *Disagree*

Some of the main concerns and problems in this area are covered in Chapter 9. But for now, consider what you would have said before the stoma operation if someone had asked you to define what makes a real man or a real woman. Perhaps you want to write down below how you think you would have answered this question.

Would you have said that you were a real man or woman and a complete person before the stoma?

I would have said I was a real man/woman before the operation
Yes/No

I would have said I was a complete person before the operation.
Yes/No

If you answer 'Yes' to one or both of these questions you can use the exercise below. If you answer 'No' to these questions, you may want to discuss how you view yourself with your nurse or doctor.

Before the operation I would have said that these things were what made me a real man/woman (it is important you try to imagine how you would have answered this before the operation):

1 ....

2 ....

3 ....

Before the operation I would have said that these things were what made me a complete person (it is important you try to imagine how you would have answered this before the operation):

1 ....

2 ....

3 ....

It will be helpful to look at your lists and see how many things have really changed. You can compare these lists with how things are for you now. Have things changed as much as you thought? Have you lost any or all of the characteristics which you would have said made you a real man/woman or a complete person? Most people who do this exercise can see that they have been focusing on the one thing that is different, and that it has been difficult to remember that there are other things which make you what you are and which haven't changed. If most of the characteristics have not changed, might it be that it is only your thoughts which have changed? Perhaps you have only been focusing on the changes since the operation, and not on the things which haven't changed? Perhaps this is making you think negatively about yourself?

Most people find that, when they think carefully about these thoughts, they still have nearly all of the factors which made them what they thought defined a 'real' man or woman, or a 'complete' person. They realize that they were not thinking about these other factors, and that thinking only about the changes was part of the problem. If you have lost some of the characteristics from your definitions, then ask yourself whether they are lost forever. Is it possible that these changes are temporary, and that there will be further change in the future? You may *feel* less like a man or a woman – but does this really mean that you *are* less of a real man or woman? Have you ever felt that something would never work out only to find that it actually did? How we feel about something is not always necessarily the case: it can be easy to confuse feelings with facts.

'I'm afraid of leakage'

Question 9: My stoma might leak if I go out. *Agree*

When you go out, you might fall and break your leg accidentally – but this doesn't usually stop you from going out. There are things that you do to reduce the risk of it happening – for example, you take care where and how you are walking when you are out. And if it did happen, there are things that you can do to get help or cope with it. Anxiety about leakage can stop you from going out at all. It is true that the stoma might leak if you go out – in the same way that you might break your leg if you go out. Does it help you to feel confident about going out, if you focus on this possibility? Would you feel confident about going for a walk if you were to dwell on the thought that you might break your leg?

There are things you can do to minimize the risk of a leak – such as making sure that your appliance is secure. You can also think of a coping plan which you can put into action if necessary. If the stoma did leak, then what is the worst thing that could happen? You might feel very embarrassed, but you would get cleaned up, people would help and life would go on. It might help if you think about what you could do to cope if you noticed you were having a leak. Remember, no one ever died of embarrassment. Have you ever been embarrassed before in life? Did it feel awkward at the time? Did you cope with it? Did it pass? Did life go on? Perhaps reminding yourself of this experience will make it easier for you to cope with worries about leaks.

'It's revolting'

Question 11: My stoma is repulsive   *Agree*

This may be true. Again, does it really make you any different from the majority of normal human beings? Most of us have a part of our

53

bodies which, at some time or other, we think is repulsive. If you often think this, and if it makes you feel very low in your spirits, then it may be a sign that you are having problems in coming to terms with your stoma. You should discuss this with your stoma-care nurse or doctor. Perhaps you only get this thought at particular times – such as when you are changing the appliance. Think of things you could do to distract yourself as a way of taking your mind off it – like imagining what you're going to do when you have finished changing it.

If your thoughts about the stoma are mostly negative, even after reading about different ways of thinking about it or after trying to change your thoughts, then this might be a sign that you are finding it difficult to get used to life with a stoma. It is important that you mention this to your doctor or stoma-care nurse so that they can talk about ways for you to get help with this. One kind of treatment – called cognitive therapy – can be helpful for anxiety and depression caused by negative thought-patterns. It helps you to identify the negative thoughts which are maintaining and feeding the anxiety and depression, and then helps you to learn ways of modifying the thoughts to make your thinking more balanced. This approach is used in the next chapter, which also includes information on the common emotional reactions to stoma surgery.

Summary

- The way in which we think about things affects the way we feel, the way we behave and our physical reactions.
- Thinking negatively about living with a stoma can make life more difficult by causing negative feelings and reactions.
- There are some common themes in stoma-related thoughts which are associated with distress and problems.
- By asking yourself some questions and thinking about your negative thoughts, you can be helped to gain another perspective on the stoma – and this in turn can help you change your feelings and behaviour.
- Changing the way you think, feel and behave about the stoma can be difficult to do on your own; you may want to speak to your doctor or nurse about referral to a specialist, such as a clinical psychologist, for help with this.

7

Coping with your feelings

Research has shown that approximately one quarter of people who have stoma operations experience serious problems with anxiety, depression and other negative emotions at some point during the year after their stoma operation. Some people who have had a stoma operation do not suffer serious problems, but may still find that there are times when they feel anxious or sad. This chapter explains some of the common features of these negative emotional reactions, and also provides information on how to develop ways of coping with such feelings. The characteristics of more serious negative emotional reactions are also outlined, as these may need to be the focus of discussion with a nurse or doctor who can arrange for professional help to improve the way you are feeling.

Anxiety

Anxiety is a common emotional reaction following stoma surgery. You may be experiencing some of the common signs and symptoms of anxiety. This does not necessarily mean that you have a major problem – it could be part of what is called a normal adjustment reaction to the big changes which have happened in your life. The common signs of anxiety can be divided into four types:

- physical sensations associated with anxiety;
- anxious thoughts;
- moods associated with anxiety;
- some of the common behavioural reactions which occur when we feel anxious.

The physical sensations which we experience as symptoms of anxiety are things like sweating, tense muscles, a pounding heart, dizziness, shortness of breath, tight chest, dry mouth, tingling and 'jelly' legs. These anxiety sensations are usually accompanied by anxious thoughts which tend to be focused on an overestimation of danger and catastrophe. These anxious thoughts are also usually related to an underestimation of your ability to cope or to obtain any help with the difficulties. The most common moods which accompany this type of thought-pattern are anxiety, fear, panic and nervousness. When people experience these moods or have anxious thoughts, they are more likely either to avoid situations in which anxiety might occur, or leave situations when they notice any of the physical sensations associated with anxiety. Try to think if you have been experiencing any of the common signs and symptoms of anxiety. If you have, then it might be helpful for you to know a bit more about anxiety and where it comes from.

Anxiety is a normal human response, designed to save our lives. Our human need to respond to stress, anxiety and fear has evolved over many thousands of years, in order to help us deal with threatening situations. Our distant ancestors faced many dangers – for example, the risk of being attacked by a sabre-toothed tiger. The human body developed a response to help us escape from such dangers – you could call it a sort of 'anxiety response'. The physical effects of anxiety mentioned above are important parts of this anxiety response – they are designed to help us and to save our lives.

The 'anxiety response' is automatically switched on when we are in a dangerous or threatening situation. Nowadays very few of us are faced with threats like sabre-toothed tigers – but we may be exposed to other dangers and threats: if you are crossing the road and a car comes screeching round the corner, speeding towards you, your heart beats faster, your breathing becomes faster, you get a churning in your stomach and you feel hot and sweaty.

This anxiety response can save your life by helping you get out of the way. Your heart beats faster to pump the blood to your muscles so that you can move quickly away from the car. You breathe faster because your heart needs more oxygen to keep it beating faster. Your muscles become very tense because you need to spring into action out of the way of the car. You have a churning sensation in your stomach because some of your blood has been directed to your legs from elsewhere in your body. Your body decides that your heart and legs need more blood for the emergency, and that your stomach can spare some of the blood which was there. You feel hot and sweaty because of all the extra work which is going on inside you – your body tries to cool down by sweating. All of these physical sensations are happening for very important reasons. Seeing the speeding car switches on the anxiety response, which helps you to escape from the danger and threat, and therefore keeps you from harm.

In this example there was a *real* danger, and it was helpful that the anxiety response was switched on. However, the anxiety response can be switched on even if we only *think* something is dangerous, threatening or difficult to cope with. You might hear a bang in the middle of the night and think that there's a burglar in your house. The anxiety response is switched on even if the noise is only your cat knocking over a plant. Your thought that it was a burglar nevertheless switched on the anxiety response. Because the response is switched on, you get a pounding heart, dizziness, churning stomach and other anxiety sensations. You might get more anxious thoughts and a desire to escape.

The anxiety response is switched on when we think about danger or not being able to cope. Thoughts about danger, catastrophe and not being able to cope commonly accompany anxious moods like fear and panic, as well as anxious behaviours like escape and avoidance. The different components of the anxiety response – physical sensations, moods, thoughts and reactions – are all connected. Making changes in one of these components has a knock-on effect on the other components. This means that if you can cope with anxious thoughts, then you will notice a difference in anxious moods and physical sensations. If you can cope with anxious behaviour, you will also be coping with anxious physical sensations and anxious thoughts. These main components of the anxiety response are outlined below.

Anxiety response: the four components

Moods:	anxiety, fear, panic.
Thoughts:	'I can't cope with this'; 'What if I never get better?'; 'What if it all goes wrong?'; 'I'm going to collapse'.
Physical sensations:	dry mouth, dizziness, chest-pain, shortness of breath, sweating, palpitations.
Behaviour:	trying to escape, avoiding things.

Panic is an extreme form of anxiety. Panic attacks are characterized by a period of intense fear, anxiety or discomfort. During a panic attack, physical sensations develop and build up to reach a peak. These sensations are usually palpitations, sweating, trembling, shortness of breath, feelings of choking, chest-pain, nausea, dizziness, feelings of unreality, tingling sensations and hot flushes. During a panic attack there is usually a feeling of impending doom (thinking that something awful is about to happen) and thoughts regarding personal catastrophe

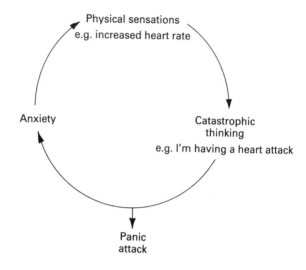

Figure 3 The vicious cycle in a panic attack

– such as, 'I am going to die'; 'I'm having a heart attack'; or, 'I'm losing my mind'. These catastrophic thoughts about the normal sensations associated with anxiety and stress make things worse – you get anxious about feeling anxious. In other words, you get a tight chest because you are uptight. You then think that the tight chest means you are having a heart attack– and this makes you feel even more anxious, which makes your chest tighten up even more. You also experience even more physical sensations, such as shortness of breath and dizziness, and become convinced that your theory that you are having a heart attack is correct. This culminates in a panic attack. Panic attacks are triggered by normal physical sensations associated with being anxious. They can also be triggered by normal sensations associated with being tired or feeling unwell.

Coping with anxiety

One of the effective ways of coping with anxiety is to learn how to identify, evaluate and then change the anxious thoughts which are part of the anxiety response. This way of coping with anxiety is outlined at the end of this chapter (pages 65–72) when we look at how to identify,

evaluate and change problem-thoughts which are caus
moods like anxiety and panic. In addition to developing ι
thinking, you can learn how to change the physical react
anxiety response. These methods of changing the anxiety re,
called relaxation techniques. There are many different tech   ω
help combat anxiety responses, some of which are outlined below.
Research suggests that, to bring about lasting changes in anxiety
problems, there have to be real and fundamental changes in thinking
patterns. However, some of these techniques may be helpful in the
short term.

Progressive muscle relaxation

One of the common relaxation techniques is called progressive muscle
relaxation, which involves learning to relax all the major muscle-
groups in your body. This combats the anxiety response because
muscle tension is a common physical sensation when we get anxious.
This technique consists of learning how to tense and then relax the
muscles of your body. You can start to learn how this works by
clenching one of your fists and holding it for about five seconds (don't
clench it too tightly – you don't want the tension to become too
painful). Then stop clenching and let all the tension go – relax your
hand. Now pay special attention to the difference between the tension
and the relaxation. Some people find it relaxing to say a soothing word
to themselves as they release the tension from their muscles – words
such as 'relax', 'let go', 'duvet' or 'release'.

When you have done this a couple of times with your fist, you are
ready to start on the main muscle-groups in your body. Work through
tensing and relaxing biceps, feet, thighs, chest, back, shoulders and
head. The aim is to help you become aware of the difference between
physical tension and relaxation. Notice the warm feelings in your fist as
you do it once more. Relaxation training is like learning any new skill –
you won't be expert at it when you begin. It will take you a couple of
weeks of regular practice before you get used to it. You will notice that
it starts to work when you set aside time to do the relaxation exercises
each day. Try not to do the relaxation exercises when you are sleepy, as
you may fall asleep. Start to notice in your everyday life when you are
physically tense (especially around your shoulders and neck-muscles).
You can then use this as your cue to release the tension from your
muscles using the progressive relaxation technique.

Another extremely effective way of relaxing is to make a list of activities which you find (or used to find) really relaxing – like having a bubble-bath, listening to a favourite piece of music or sitting stroking the cat. You can make sure that you do at least three of these each day – or alternatively, you can do one of these activities when you are feeling particularly tense or anxious to combat the anxiety response.

Breathing re-training

When the anxiety response is switched on, our breathing is affected, and we breathe in an unbalanced way – that is, we upset the balance of oxygen and carbon dioxide in our blood. This is one of the main reasons why people experience physical sensations such as dizziness, and have a funny, tingling sensation at the end of their fingers (paraesthesia). It is easy to get your breathing back into balance again by trying not to take large gasps of air. Instead, you can try to retrain your breathing pattern to get a balance. Start to notice your breathing pattern, and whether or not it is unbalanced – if it is, you can take steps to regulate your breathing pattern. Just as unbalanced breathing was a habit, you can make a more balanced breathing pattern become a habit. To begin learning this skill, practise breathing in for the count of four (think '1', '2', '3', '4' as you breathe in), and then breathe out for the count of four.

We have already seen the benefits of distraction in keeping your mind occupied and focused away from worrying thoughts about medical tests. You can also use distraction to cope with the physical reactions of the anxiety response. Distraction techniques are helpful for anxiety responses because they focus your mind away from the anxious thoughts which maintain anxious moods, behaviours and physical reactions.

Anti-anxiety drugs

Sometimes doctors prescribe tablets to help people cope with an anxiety response. Some of the common anti-anxiety drugs are diazepam; propranolol; and buspirone. Most anti-anxiety drugs are prescribed only as a short-term measure, because research has shown that some of them can become addictive. We also know that, when someone takes certain anti-anxiety drugs for a long period of time, they need to take more and more to get the same effect. Drugs only take away the physical sensations – and the anxious thoughts and behaviour usually return when the drugs are stopped. This is not always the case, and you should always discuss your individual situation with a doctor. Anti-anxiety drugs may be a useful first-aid measure for anxiety symptoms – but they are not a long-term answer to anxiety for most people.

Serious anxiety problems

If you are experiencing some of the signs and symptoms mentioned above, then you may be suffering from an anxiety disorder which could benefit from specialist help. If you are feeling anxious, having physical anxiety symptoms, anxious thoughts and worries most days, or if any of these symptoms are especially unpleasant and uncontrollable, you should mention this to your nurse or doctor. You should also mention if you have had panic attacks and keep worrying that you will have another one. It is especially important that you have specialist help if you have noticed that you are avoiding situations, or have developed special rituals to protect you from experiencing the anxiety symptoms. There are effective treatments available for most anxiety disorders.

Depression

As we saw earlier, the anxiety response has four components – thoughts, behaviour, physical sensations and moods. Depression – a reaction sometimes experienced following stoma surgery – can be similarly described. The most obvious mood experienced by someone with depression is sadness – though irritability, guilt and despair can also be problem-moods in depression. Depressed people tend to have negative thoughts about themselves (such as, 'I am a failure'; 'I am useless'; 'I am unattractive'), about the world (such as, 'Other people do not like me'), and about the future (such as, 'Things will never get any better'). When someone is depressed, their behaviour changes. They stop doing things that they used to enjoy doing, they feel tired most of the time, they have problems with sleep and may cry a lot of the time.

Coping with depression

There are a number of simple and effective strategies, outlined below, which can be used to combat depression and the behavioural patterns which are part of feeling depressed.

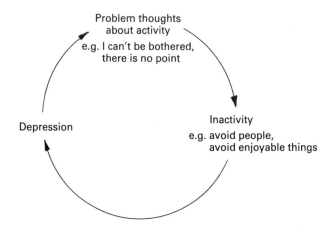

Figure 4 The vicious cycle in depression

Planning activities

When someone is troubled by depression they start to do less and less. Someone who is depressed is less active in general, and stops doing the things which they used to enjoy. This reduced activity-level can be caused by problem-thoughts such as, 'There's no point', 'I can't be bothered', or 'I won't enjoy it'. Because of this negative thought-pattern, depressed people will not do anything, and they thus become more and more inactive and more and more depressed. This can become a vicious cycle which maintains the depressed mood, actions and thought-patterns.

One way of dealing with this problem and breaking the vicious cycle is to start gradually to increase the number of pleasurable activities you do in a day. Start off by doing one pleasurable activity each day, and then build this up until you are doing approximately ten pleasurable activities each week. It can be helpful to start by thinking about all the things you used to enjoy doing, and making a list of them. You can then pick from this list which one you will try first. You don't need to do a time-consuming or expensive activity – anything enjoyable will do. You may be tempted to compare your pleasure with what it used to be like for you – but try not to do this. Focus on the pleasure that you're getting now, and how this is better than sitting around doing nothing or avoiding opportunities for enjoyment. You will find that if you can break this vicious cycle then your mood will gradually lift. You might also be surprised to find that many of the problem-thoughts about not enjoying things, or there being no point in doing anything, were not true at all.

Serious depression problems

As you read this book, you may be worrying that depression is more than a passing feeling or that it is a big problem for you. It may be that you have some of the signs and symptoms of what is called a major depressive episode, or clinical depression. If this is true, then there are many effective treatments from which you can benefit (such as antidepressant drugs or cognitive therapy).

How many of the following symptoms have you experienced in the past fortnight?

- feeling depressed all day every day, and not being able to 'snap out of it';
- not enjoying or getting pleasure from anything you do;
- having problems with sleeping (not getting off to sleep or waking up very early);
- having difficulties in concentrating or making decisions;
- thinking about death or killing yourself;
- feeling guilty or worthless;
- having a poor appetite or not enjoying your food as much as you used to.

If you have had four or more of the above signs or symptoms in the past two weeks, then it may be that you are experiencing a clinically significant problem with depression. You should discuss this with your family doctor for a more detailed assessment as soon as you can.

Antidepressant drugs

Antidepressant drugs are not addictive. They take approximately three weeks before they are effective, and they usually need to be taken for six months after you start to feel better. Taking them in this way means that there will be less chance that the depression will return. Common examples of antidepressant drugs are fluoxetine, amitryptiline, dothie-pin, citalopram, sertraline, paroxetine, lofepramine and trazodone – all of which are often known by their trade-names.

Suicidal thoughts

Sometimes people who are suffering from depression feel that life is not worth living, or that they would be better off dead. If you have been having such thoughts, then it is important that you speak to your doctor or nurse about this. This can be a symptom of depression and can be treated. People usually start thinking about suicide when they cannot think of any other way to solve their problems, or because they think that there are more advantages to being dead. These thoughts are always the result of distorted or biased thought-processes. If you have been thinking that life is not worth living, then it can be helpful to remind yourself of reasons for living. There will have been a time in your life when you thought that life was worth living – what were your reasons for living at that time? Try to remember that these suicidal thoughts are symptoms of an illness which can be helped by treatment if you speak to your doctor.

Dealing with feelings by changing our thoughts

As we saw in the last chapter, the way we think about things is very important in understanding why we experience particular feelings, what we do and what our physical reactions are. Because of this link between thoughts, emotions, behaviour and physical reactions, it can have very dramatic effects if we change the way we think about things – altering our unhelpful feelings, actions and physical reactions associated with anxiety or depression. These are the basic principles behind a psychological treatment called cognitive therapy. Cognitive therapy is a 'talking treatment' which aims to help the patient understand how thinking patterns may be affecting their feelings and behaviour. The patient and cognitive therapist work together to make sense of the problem-feelings and actions, and then work on changing problem-thought-patterns. Cognitive therapy has been shown to be effective in helping people who suffer from anxiety disorders or clinical depression. If you are interested in finding out more about it, there are details of further reading in the 'Useful information' section at the end of the book. The rest of this chapter outlines some of the basics in helping you to identify, evaluate and change the problem-thoughts which create and feed negative and unhelpful moods, actions and physical reactions.

There are two main steps to helping yourself with your problem-thought-patterns:

1 Identifying what thoughts are causing you problems.
2 Evaluating and changing the way in which you think about certain events or situations.

Identifying problem-thoughts

Before you can identify a problem-thought, you need to identify the mood which accompanies it and which you would like to change. This poses no problems for some people. However, others find it difficult to know what feeling or emotion they are experiencing, and how to describe it. It can be helpful to spend a few days 'tuning in' to your emotions. You can do this by making a mental note of what emotion you are experiencing at different points during the day. Ask yourself, 'What am I feeling right now?' You may find it helpful to look at the emotion checklist below, as you start to become aware of and tune in to your emotions.

Emotion checklist

This checklist includes negative emotions. Look at the checklist to see if you can identify any negative emotions which bother you, and which you might want to change by changing your thinking patterns:

- worry
- anxiety
- depression
- anger
- frustration
- fear
- panic
- irritability
- shame
- guilt
- sadness

After you have spent some time tuning in to your emotions, you will notice that you experience many different moods – some positive, some negative; some which are strong emotions and others which do not have as much of a grip on you. It is probably the strong negative emotions that you want to learn to cope with. Throughout this book I have recommended writing things down. Writing down information about your feelings and thoughts can be helpful because it can remind you of the details of how you were feeling, or what you were thinking about. This is necessary if you want to develop ways of changing your problem-thoughts in order to cope with strong negative emotional reactions, such as anxiety or depression.

If you notice a negative mood (e.g. depression), then try to think about how strong that negative mood is. In other words, try to give it a score from 0 to 100 per cent. A score of 0 would mean not depressed at all, while a score of 100 per cent would mean the most depressed that you could ever imagine feeling. Can you think of a strong negative mood that you have had recently? Try to score how strong it was using a 0–100 per cent scale. Scoring the negative mood is an important part of identifying and changing your problem-thoughts. This is because mood-ratings can be made before and after your attempt to change your problem-thoughts, in order to check how big the mood-improvement is.

When you start to notice negative moods which you want to change, you are ready to start looking for problem-thoughts. Negative moods are always accompanied by problem-thoughts. When you notice that you are having a strong negative mood (e.g. depressed: 85 per cent), write this down on a Problem-Thought Record (there is an example towards the end of this chapter). Write down a brief description of the situation you are in when the negative mood happens: Where are you? Who else is there? What are you doing or saying?

You can now start to find the problem-thought which is behind the negative mood. The best way to find problem-thoughts is to ask yourself some simple questions. These are tried-and-tested questions to help you identify the problem-thought which is behind your strong negative feeling. Remember that it is problem-thoughts which make problem-moods stay with you. If you can learn to identify the problem-thoughts then you are well on the way to coping with the problem-moods.

Questions for identifying problem-thoughts

Whenever you experience a problem-mood ask yourself these questions to help you identify the problem-thoughts behind it:

1 What was going through my mind just as I started to have this problem-mood?
2 What does this situation mean to me? What does this situation say about me?
3 What is the worst thing that could happen in this situation?
4 What have I just been thinking about?
5 What do I guess that I was thinking about just then?

Write down the answers to these questions on the Problem-Thought Record. Your answers to the questions will contain the problem-thoughts which are feeding into the problem-mood. When you have identified a list of problem-thoughts, you can try to modify them to create a more helpful way of thinking about things. It has been shown that, when you keep using this technique, strong moods become less intense (e.g. 'depressed: 85 per cent' becomes 'depressed: 25 per cent'), and you experience the negative moods less often. Because moods are linked to actions and physical reactions there is also a knock-on effect – changing thoughts changes moods which change actions and physical reactions. In order to modify the problem-thoughts, you need to try to get a different perspective. To do this, you can learn to ask yourself some different questions – questions which are designed to change the problem-thought.

Common thinking biases

Problem-thoughts are often the result of biases or distortions in thinking. These biases or distortions have special names. When you come to change problem-thoughts it can be helpful to look for these biases. Some of the common biases are described below.

All-or-nothing thinking: seeing things in black-and-white categories – either everything is going completely well or it is a complete disaster. There are no shades of grey when this type of thinking-bias is operating. An example of all-or-nothing thinking would be, 'These stoma bags are completely useless.'

Over-generalization: seeing a single event as part of a never-ending pattern of events or generalizing from one isolated event to the rest of our lives. Thoughts such as, 'My bag always leaks when I go out', when you have experienced one leak; or, 'Everything is going wrong with my stoma', when you get an area of sore skin – these are examples of thoughts which are a result of over-generalization.

Mental filter: picking out a single negative detail and focusing on it exclusively. An example of this would be focusing on, 'The surgeon said I might develop some problems later on', and forgetting that he also said that this was unlikely and that there were many effective treatments if problems did develop.

Discounting the positive: saying that positive experiences don't count. If you are feeling that your energy-levels are increasing after surgery, you might say to yourself, 'So what? I am still apprehensive about going out and meeting people.' This is an example of discounting the positive.

Jumping to conclusions: drawing conclusions when there are no facts to support your conclusion. 'Mind-reading' is an example of this – you make predictions about what other people think as if you had mind-reading abilities. Thoughts such as, 'They are not interested in visiting me', or, 'They think that I smell', are examples of this. 'Fortune-telling' is another bias which involves jumping to conclusions. This involves predicting that something won't work out – 'I'll never get used to this stoma', or, 'Swimming will never be the same again', are examples of the fortune-telling bias. You think these thoughts as if you can really see into the future.

Magnification: exaggerating the importance of your difficulties and problems, and minimizing your abilities to cope and your positive qualities. A thought like, 'Being more confident about the appliance is no big deal – I still feel awkward wearing it', is the result of the magnification bias.

Emotional reasoning: assuming that our negative feelings are a reflection of the way that things really are. You may be saying to yourself, 'I feel that everyone is looking at me', or, 'I feel that people can see my stoma through my clothes'. This bias causes us to confuse feelings with facts. Because you feel a certain way you believe that it is that way.

Personalization: holding yourself personally responsible for an event which is not entirely under your control. You may think, 'The doctor only spoke to me for a few minutes because I was not explaining things clearly', when the doctor might simply have been busier than usual.

Questions for changing problem-thoughts

When you have written down the situation, the problem-mood and the problem-thoughts, you can start to try to change the thoughts as a way of improving the way you feel. Just as you can identify problem-thoughts by asking yourself a set of questions, so you can also modify your problem-thoughts by asking yourself a series of questions. When you have identified the problem-thoughts and written them down on the Problem-Thought Record, ask yourself the questions listed below. Write your answers on the Problem-Thought Record as 'More helpful and alternative thoughts'.

1 What experiences have I had which show me that this thought is not completely true all of the time?
2 If I were trying to help someone I cared about to feel better when they had this thought, what would I tell them?
3 What advice might someone I cared about give to me if they knew that I was thinking about things in this way? Would they agree with me? If not, why not?
4 When I am not experiencing this problem-mood, how would I think about things?
5 What have I learned from previous events or experiences in my life which might help me to cope with this problem-thought?
6 Is my problem-thought an example of a thinking-bias? If so, which one is it?
7 What is the evidence to support this thought? What is the evidence against this thought?
8 What is the worst thing that could happen? Could I live through and cope with this?
9 What is the best thing that could happen? What is the most realistic outcome?
10 What would be the effect of changing this problem-thought? What can I do now?

You should now have a better idea about how to identify problem-situations and moods. This chapter ends with an example of a completed Problem-Thought Record; there are also some blank Problem-Thought Records for you to fill in and practise on. If you want to find out more about using these techniques, then you can get a copy of *Mind Over Mood* (details in the 'Further reading' section at the end of the book).

Problem-Thought Record – Example
Day/Date/Situation

Monday, 25 March
Sitting watching TV programme about operations

Problem-mood(s)

depressed: *65 per cent*
frustrated: *50 per cent*

My problem-thoughts
(This is where you write answers to the questions which help you identify problem-thoughts)

I can't be bothered getting dressed.
I will never get over this operation and be normal again.
I have no energy to visit Mark today – I'll not enjoy it anyway.

My more helpful and alternative thoughts
(This is where you write answers to the questions which help you to see things differently)

If someone I knew thought this, I would advise them to get dressed – they would feel better once they did it.

I am predicting the future in a negative way and this isn't going to help me.

When I don't feel this way, I would think that I just need to take it easy and one step at a time – be kind to myself.

My thoughts are affected by biases like fortune-telling and emotional reasoning – I can try to reverse these biases.

If I try, then I might get some energy. I don't know for sure that I won't enjoy it until I try.

Problem-moods now

depressed:	*20 per cent*
frustrated:	*10 per cent*

Problem-Thought Record
Day/Date/Situation

Problem-mood(s)

My problem-thoughts

My more helpful and alternative thoughts

Problem-moods now

Problem-Thought Record
Day/Date/Situation

Problem-mood(s)

My problem-thoughts

My more helpful and alternative thoughts

Problem-moods now

Summary

- Anxiety is a common reaction following a stoma operation and can be understood by looking at its four components (physical sensations, moods, thoughts and actions). Anxiety is characterized by physical sensations such as dizziness and dry mouth; moods such as fear and panic; thoughts such as, 'I can't cope with this', and, 'I'm going to collapse', and actions such as avoidance and escape.
- The human anxiety response developed to save us from danger, but can also be switched on when we think that a situation is dangerous, even if it isn't.
- Anxiety responses can be dealt with using strategies such as breathing retraining and progressive muscle relaxation; anti-anxiety drugs may also be used as a short-term measure.
- Depression can also be understood in terms of four components – physical sensations, such as loss of appetite; moods, such as sadness and irritability; thoughts, such as, 'I'm a failure', and, 'Life is a mess'; and actions such as withdrawing from others and becoming inactive.
- Depression can be helped by gradually increasing activity-levels and planning enjoyable activities which give a sense of achievement. Antidepressant medication may also be helpful for some people.
- Clinical depression is more serious, and requires consultation with your GP.
- Problem-thoughts are one of the main reasons why negative moods become problems after stoma surgery. You can learn some simple techniques for identifying emotions and problem-thoughts, and for modifying the problem-thoughts to help you feel better.

8

Dealing with social situations

Some of the most common concerns of people with a stoma are about social and public situations. You may have been worrying that the bag will come off or leak when you're in a public situation, that the stoma will make embarrassing noises when you least expect it, that it will give off an unpleasant smell or that other people will notice your bag underneath your clothing. Some of these thoughts have already been mentioned – but this chapter provides some specific advice about worries regarding social situations, and outlines three particular techniques which can be used to deal with such concerns.

Worries about the stoma being detected, and other people thinking negatively about you, can make it difficult to get used to being in social situations after your operation. Moira had an ileostomy and was afraid that her stoma would give off a foul smell or make an unexpected noise if she went to visit Mike. She thought that she couldn't possibly cope with this. She also believed that Mike would think she was dirty and rude if he noticed the smell or heard the noise. Because of these thoughts she felt anxious, dizzy and tense, and her heart was racing. She decided to avoid visiting Mike.

Moira's worries about this social situation are maintained by her thought that she'll have a problem if she visits Mike, that she won't be able to cope with the problem if it occurs, and that Mike will think less of her because of the problem. It is not surprising that she doesn't go to visit Mike, and that she feels anxiety sensations as a result of these problem-thoughts. Yet Moira could modify these problem-thoughts by using a Problem-Thought Record. This is likely to be helpful as there are a number of thinking-biases in her thoughts about this social situation. What do you think are Moira's main thinking-biases?

In addition to focusing on the thoughts which underlie the desire to avoid social situations and the worries about such situations, it is possible to use some different techniques to cope with this. It is all too easy to focus on the worst possible scenario, and to underestimate what you could do to cope if the worst were to happen. You keep thinking that this *will* happen (though you may be overestimating the chances) – and stop there. You don't think further about whether there would be anything you could really do to cope if it did happen.

What is the worst thing that can happen?

Social anxiety usually occurs when you believe that something will go wrong in a social situation. You may worry that your stoma will make a noise or that you will smell. You may imagine that your bag is leaking all over your clothing in the middle of the supermarket, or that noises might come from the bag during prayers at church. It is natural to have these sorts of worries after your stoma operation. However, such worries can become a problem if you start to feel really apprehensive and to avoid doing things you enjoy. This can be one of the first signs of clinical depression.

Think for a moment about what is the worst thing that could happen to you. Try to think about it in as much detail as possible. What would happen? How would you feel? What would your stoma be doing? What would you say? What would other people be doing? Now that you have an idea about the worst-case scenario, ask yourself if this is likely to happen. Might you be overestimating how likely it is? How many times have you been in similar situations and been OK?

'I couldn't cope if that happened'

Now that you have thought about the worst-case scenario, you will probably see that you have been overestimating the likelihood of the worst happening. This exercise might also have triggered thoughts and worries that you could not possibly cope if this were to happen. Accidents and unplanned incidents do happen. Instead of assuming that you couldn't cope, why not make a coping-plan now, before it happens? Instead of stopping after you have thought about the worst possibility, take it forward and construct a coping-plan.

Write down your worst-case scenario for a social situation on the left-hand side of a piece of paper, and then on the right-hand side of the same piece of paper write down what you could do to cope if this were to happen. This might be difficult, but you can try to make it easier by thinking about what other people might do to cope – or by asking some people you trust about what they might do. This exercise helps you to see that there are things which you could do to cope if your fears were to come true. Not only that, but you are also thinking about a coping-plan in advance so that if something awful did happen, you would be prepared in advance. You wouldn't have to think on the spot – you would have worked it all out beforehand. In other words, you just put the coping-plan into action as you have prepared it. This technique can also be used for worst-case scenarios in other areas of life – such as future illness, family problems or staying with friends. I know some couples who devise a special code word to indicate to each other that an accident has occurred. Some examples of worst-case scenarios with coping plans are outlined below.

Worst-case scenario	Coping-plan
The bag will come off and the contents start to run down my leg.	*I can excuse myself and go to the bathroom to clean myself up. I can then go home and change.*
Norma will ask me about my stoma when I do not want to talk about it.	*I can say that I appreciate her concerns but that I am not ready to talk about my stoma to other people yet.*
The stoma will make loud noises when everyone is quiet, and I will feel so embarrassed.	*I could say, 'Oh – excuse me', when this happens; or I could say when I arrive that my operation means that my bowel can sometimes make noises. I can remind myself that people have previously been really understanding.*
The stoma will balloon with air and there will be a bulge in my dress. There might be a smell.	*I can go to the bathroom and let the air out. I can remind myself that it is unlikely that anyone else will have noticed.*

Remember that, even if your fears were to come true, there is something you could do to cope with the events. Most likely you will never need to use the coping-plan – but at least you know it is there if you were to need it. Most people say that they find it easier to put into action a plan which they've already thought about – rather than having to create a plan when something happens. You can use the space below to write down your worst-case scenario and your coping-plan for this.

Worst-case scenario **\|** *Coping-plan*

'I don't know what to tell other people'

Some of my patients have coped with worries about telling other people about their stoma by practising what to say to them. In this way, they can think of how to say it and take control of the social situation. Some, for example, find it helpful to explain about their stoma as soon as they enter a new social situation. One man told me that this was his, way of making sure that other people knew what was happening if there was an embarrassing noise. This might seem difficult, but once you have thought out what you want to say to someone, you can practise it beforehand. Many people would prefer not to say anything – but this strategy of planning and practising what to say may be the key to reducing your worries about what others will think.

Here is an example of what one patient felt comfortable saying:

'As you know, I have been very ill. To save my life I had a colostomy operation – that means I have to wear a bag on my tummy. It sometimes makes some funny noises – which can be a bit embarrassing. I hope you don't mind me saying, but I feel less anxious if I explain in advance.'

He found that most people were extremely understanding when he said this.

It is unlikely that other people will either notice the bag or any smell that it gives off (other people's noses are much further away from it than yours). Stoma patients who have come to my clinic with social anxiety seem to think that their friends and acquaintances are not going to be understanding. However, they then tell me that they themselves would understand if someone they knew had had a stoma. If you have explained to someone about your operation, how could they possibly not be understanding of the fact that you have experienced a major, life-saving operation?

Action not avoidance

You might be scared about going out on long journeys to see friends, or staying for a while at someone's house. This is probably because you have lost some control over your bowel or bladder. One way to overcome this is with a gradual approach, whereby you work gently towards getting back to the way you were before the operation. In other words, you don't have to jump in at the deep end – your first outing after the operation doesn't have to be a big social occasion, like a local coffee-morning or the golf club dinner-dance – but you can work up to this slowly. This is a very important technique for dealing with anxiety-provoking situations, and is called 'graded exposure'.

Here is an example of the graded-exposure steps made by one stoma patient who was feeling anxious about going out because of her appliance.

Final goal: Go to Sheila's coffee-morning

Step	Description	Anxiety rating (0–10)		
		predicted	*actual*	*date(s)*
1	Go into the corner shop	6	4	4 June
		5	3	5 June
2	Visit Doreen	8	4	6 June
3	Go to the post office	7	3	8 June
		5	3	9 June
4	Go to the supermarket	4	2	9 June
		4	2	10 June
5	Go to Sheila's coffee-morning	5	1	13 June

This woman thought about what she wanted to be able to do (go to the coffee-morning on 13 June), and then devised a plan to help her work towards this gradually. If you think that this technique might be helpful, then first of all think about what activity you would like to be able to do. Then try to break it down into smaller steps – and when you have done this, you are ready to start your gradual approach to reaching your goal. The idea is to keep repeating a step until you feel comfortable enough to move on to the next step. By keeping a note of how anxious she thought she would be and how anxious she actually was, this woman could also see that she was overestimating her anxiety levels. She was fortune-telling, in terms of her thinking-bias. Every time you do a step, keep a note of how anxious you thought you would be beforehand, and how anxious you actually were. Remember that the key is to keep repeating each step until you are ready for the next one. If you move on too quickly, don't worry – just go back to the previous step until you feel ready to move on. You might also want to think of a more gradual step forward, in case your step was too ambitious.

Final goal: ....

Step	Description	Anxiety rating (0–10)		
		Predicted	Actual	Dates
1				
2				
3				
4				
5				

Becoming less self-conscious

You might notice that, since the operation, you have become acutely self-conscious, with your attention completely focused on your stoma and how you are feeling physically. This means that you are more aware of it, and thus more prone to start thinking that the stoma will make a noise and/or smell. You can cope with this self-conscious tendency by really trying to direct your attention to what is going on around you. This helps, because you become less aware of the stoma and what it is up to. One way of directing your attention away from your bodily sensations is to focus on what other people are wearing, what they are saying, whether you like their clothes, hairstyles, etc.

Your anxiety about social situations may be so overpowering that you find it difficult to overcome. It may be interfering with your usual routine – your return to work and/or your social life. Indeed, it may be so bad that you stay in all the time, or that you have a panic attack in social situations. If this sounds like you, discuss it with your stoma-care nurse or GP. They may think that you should see a clinical psychologist about this more serious form of social anxiety.

Summary

- Worries about stoma smells or noises can make social situations really difficult to cope with.
- Recording your thoughts in social situations, and developing an alternative way of thinking, can help you to feel less anxious in social situations.
- Thinking about possible problems (the worst-case scenario), and how to cope with them in advance, is an excellent way of preparing for your worst fears.
- Explaining to other people about the stoma can make you less worried about what they might think if you have a problem with the stoma while you're with them.
- If you feel anxious about a social situation, you could take a gradual approach, starting with a quiet situation and then building up to a busier one.
- Switching the focus of your attention away from yourself to the situation can be an effective way of dealing with self-consciousness (your tendency to focus on the stoma).

9
Sex, intimacy and stomas

'My initial concerns about my stoma related to its appearance, and the worries I had about intimacy. I was very aware of the pouch, even the mini-pouch which is available. My fears were conveyed to my partner, resulting in less intimacy between us. It took longer than I expected to get used to this' (Female with ileostomy, aged 40).

Human beings often find it difficult to talk openly about sexual matters and intimate relationships. Healthcare professionals are human beings and, despite the fact that they may have had some training in this area, they may also find it difficult to talk to their patients about sex and intimacy. This is unfortunate, as life with a stoma inevitably means that intimate relationships are an issue which stoma patients want to talk about at some stage before or after the operation. This chapter outlines some of the main issues which affect the intimate relationships of people with stomas. First, we will look at the worries which stoma patients may have as to what to say to a new partner about their stoma; and then at the worries which people may develop about the effect of the stoma on an existing relationship. The chapter then focuses on human sexual responses, some of the problems which can develop following a stoma operation, and some strategies which can be used to overcome problems in this area.

Sex and intimacy have different degrees of importance in people's lives. This may not be an area of major concern for you – and because of this, you may not need to read this chapter. Some readers may be shocked by the explicit nature of parts of this chapter – but to shock is not my intention. I make no apology for highlighting sex and intimacy as an important part of life with a stoma. I have encountered too many patients who did not receive appropriate information on this aspect of their lives because healthcare professionals could not overcome their own embarrassment. I also know of patients who were afraid to ask for details, and staff who made sweeping generalizations about a particular patient's life (such as, 'They won't be interested in that sort of thing at their age').

What shall I tell a future partner?

If you are not in an intimate relationship before stoma surgery, you may be very worried about how you will tell a potential partner about your stoma. Most people in this situation find it difficult to know whether to tell about the stoma right from the moment they meet someone to whom they are attracted, or whether to wait until there is a possibility of sexual intimacy. Some people are surprised to find out that, after weeks of worrying about what to say, when to say it and how, their new partner already knows about it from a friend or relative. Remember that most people do not even know what a stoma is. This can be an advantage, as they will take their lead from you. If you tell them about it in a matter-of-fact way which suggests that you have no problems with it, then they will have nothing to be concerned about. They will see that you are not concerned – and therefore that they do not need to be either. Everyone has a different way of dealing with this potentially awkward situation.

The important thing is to think about all the options open to you, and to weigh up the advantages and disadvantages of each one in advance. This is called a cost-benefit analysis. If you are finding it difficult to decide what to say to a future partner, then you can think of the advantages and disadvantages of some of the options listed below. Beside each option write down what you see as its advantages and disadvantages. This will help you decide what looks best for you.

Cost-benefit analysis

Options	*Advantages*	*Disadvantages*
1 Do not tell them about it at all.		
2 Tell them if I feel the relationship developing in that way.		
3 Wait until the last possible minute – when they need to know.		

Most people decide that telling a potential partner as soon as possible is the preferred option. Their reasons for this strategy are that, if they feel warmly towards someone, then they would like to find out as soon as possible how their potential partner feels about the stoma. This way they can avoid being hurt too much, because the relationship is in the early stages. However, you may wish to think of another strategy – one which may be better for you, and right for the particular life-situation or potential partner. You might want to think about 'rehearsing' your preferred option to make it easier when the situation actually arises. You might even want to go over what you plan to say with a friend, or with someone you know well – this can be helpful because it lets you try out different ways of saying things, and can boost your confidence about how to tell the other person.

Once you have decided on your preferred option, you can then think about all of the other person's possible responses. You will then be prepared for whatever happens – rather than having to think of an instant response to what they do or say. Suppose that you have completed the cost-benefit analysis and have decided to tell your potential partner about your stoma when you feel that the relationship is developing in a positive direction. You can now think about all the possible responses this option may prompt and how you will deal with each one.

For example:

Chosen option	Possible reaction	What I'll do
Tell him when I feel the relationship is going that way.	He will say nothing about it, and change the subject.	I can say that it is important to me to talk about how he feels about it.
	He says he already knew about it because my friend told him.	I can ask him how he feels about it.

Most people report positive experiences of telling other people about their stoma. Common reactions are, 'Is that all?'; or, 'What are you telling me that for – I'm not bothered'; or, 'I don't care about that, I love you as a person'. However, it is important to remember that there is a remote possibility that the person you tell may not wish to continue with the relationship. Obviously you hope that this will not happen.

But the possibility must be mentioned, as rejection of this kind can be a crushing blow – especially if you have had to deal with rejections before, or if you have a negative view of yourself. If the person does not wish the relationship to continue, then it might be helpful to consider whether it is better to find out at this stage instead of months later. Would you really have wanted to continue in a relationship with someone who is so bothered by the stoma? Try not to start thinking that you must be flawed as a person, and that this means that you will never have a relationship again in the future. You might want to talk this experience over with a trusted friend, if it does happen.

Will my present partner reject me?

If you were already involved in an intimate relationship before having stoma surgery, you may have worried about its effects on your relationship – that your partner would not find you attractive following surgery, or would reject you. Whatever your concerns about the effect of the stoma on your relationship, try to talk them over with each other. You may be surprised to find that this is enough in itself to make you both feel better about the situation. You might also want to talk things over with someone whom you feel you can confide in – perhaps a friend, a relative or one of the health professionals you know, such as the stoma-care nurse, practice nurse or your GP. Sometimes, worries about rejection by a partner can be a reflection of thoughts you are having about yourself – such as, I feel unattractive. These thoughts are not usually what other people actually think about you. If you are thinking this way you probably have the thinking-bias of mind-reading – accepting that your partner thinks this way without even discussing it with them.

It can be easy to focus on only one piece of information and blow it out of proportion – you might want to use a Problem-Thought Record (Chapter 7) to identify the problem-thoughts behind the problem-feelings in your relationship. You may have noticed that you have become very self-conscious, preferring to get undressed in the dark, avoiding mirrors, diving under the bed-covers to avoid being seen, or locking the bathroom door to avoid your partner seeing you. Some people find that their stoma adds to relationship difficulties which were already present before the operation was carried out. In my experience, relationship breakdown following stoma surgery is almost always due to problems which were already in the relationship before the operation. Relationship problems may benefit from professional help, such as marriage counselling.

Sexual aspects of relationships

Whether or not you were involved in a relationship before the stoma operation, you probably have some questions or concerns about intimacy, and the sexual aspects of your relationship. First, we will look at the basic elements of human sexual responses, and then at some of the sexual problems which can occur following stoma surgery. Some details on strategies to help with concerns regarding intimacy and sexual problems will then be discussed.

The human sexual response

Masters and Johnson, two famous researchers in the area of human sexual behaviour, worked out that our sexual responses can be divided into five main stages. These stages are characterized by desire, excitement, plateau, orgasm and resolution. It is helpful to understand the main features of these five stages of the human sexual response before considering some of the common problems which can follow a stoma operation.

- The 'desire' stage of the human sexual response is characterized by thoughts, fantasies and urges to engage in sexual activity. You are experiencing this stage if you are 'in the mood' for sex. Sexual desire can be triggered by internal or external cues. An example of an external cue is seeing your partner naked after a shower, or smelling a favourite fragrance which you associate with them. An example of an internal cue is thinking about cuddling your partner or a pleasant event which you have both shared in the past.
- The next stage of the human sexual response is called the 'excitement' stage. During this stage various physical changes occur within the body which enable sexual intercourse to take place (assuming this is desired by both partners). In men this stage is characterized by increased blood-flow to the penis (the penis lengthens, becoming hard and erect) and a general increase in overall physical arousal which causes increased blood-pressure, heart-rate and breathing-rate. In women the sexual excitement stage is characterized by the same general increase in overall arousal, and by increased blood-flow to the vagina. The vagina also lengthens.

- The 'excitement' stage of the human sexual response is followed by the 'plateau' stage, when there is a levelling-off of arousal. It is during this third stage that men experience what is called 'ejaculatory inevitability'. This means that the man knows that he is going to ejaculate (or 'come').
- The fourth stage of the human sexual response is orgasm. During this stage the woman experiences a sense of intense pleasure, accompanied by rhythmic contractions of the muscles around the base of the vagina. In a man the orgasm stage is when rhythmic contractions of the urethra (see Chapter 2) propel semen (sperm) outwards.
- The fifth and final stage of the human sexual response is called the 'resolution' stage. In both men and women this stage is characterized by a general calming down and a feeling of relaxation. In men there is a rapid loss of erection, and for a period of time there is little response to further stimulation. Further ejaculation is impossible (the 'refractory period').

You probably recognize these stages from your own sexual experiences currently or in the past. Knowing about these stages in the human sexual response makes it easier to understand some of the problems which can develop, as you can pinpoint the stage at which the problem is happening.

Sexual intimacy after stoma surgery

For different people, sexual intimacy has different degrees of importance. Most people find that, with time, they forget about the stoma during sexual intimacy. You may have experienced having to wear glasses for the first time, or having a new hairstyle. Initially you are very conscious about it, but as time goes on you notice that you (and other people) become less aware of the change. This process is called habituation. The same thing happens with your self-consciousness about the stoma and the appliance during intimacy.

Remember that you have had major surgery, and that you should resume sexual activity gradually. It is probably best to wait until your abdominal wound has healed before you engage in full sexual intercourse again. It is a good idea to ensure that the appliance is emptied before sexual intimacy, and that it is securely in place. You may also want to consider wearing a smaller appliance at this time if it is possible. Some people roll their appliance upwards and tape it to their abdomen to stop it getting in the way. Appliance-covers can be bought to camouflage the pouch, and may help if you are concerned about this.

A partner may be worried that the stoma will be damaged during sexual intimacy. You can reassure them that this is not the case. The stoma should never be used as part of sexual activity (for example, attempting to insert fingers or a penis into the stoma). If you are worried about intercourse, then perhaps as a couple you can have an agreement that, to start with, you will restrict your intimate moments to hugging, kissing and touching. This way the pressure is off, and you don't need to worry that things are going to progress too fast for you. It can sometimes be helpful to remember (especially in the early stages after surgery) that there is more to intimacy than sexual intercourse (baths, showers, massage, kissing, cuddling etc.). Patience, communication and mutual understanding are the key components to overcoming concerns about sexual intimacy following surgery. Expect some awkward moments and a few setbacks. Try to see these as opportunities for you to grow closer together as a couple.

All the information in this chapter applies equally to heterosexual and homosexual intimacy. The issues and facts relating to lesbian sex and gay male sex are exactly the same – the stoma need not be an obstacle to a satisfying and mutually fulfilling sexual relationship. Some men who have had a stoma operation may have undergone an abdominoperineal resection (see Chapter 2), in which their rectum and anal passage are closed. If a man has previously enjoyed anal intercourse with a partner, then this may be a difficult part of adjusting to life with a stoma. (There is a tendency for heterosexuals to assume that men who have sex with men only ever engage in anal intercourse. This illustrates a common problem in understanding sexual intimacy – never make assumptions.) Most men who have sex with men can enjoy pleasurable and fulfilling sexual relationships by other means after stoma surgery such as oral sex and mutual masturbation.

Sexual problems after stoma surgery

Stoma surgery can involve the risk of damaging nerves in the body which are involved in sexual functioning. If you have not been given information about whether this applies to you, contact your stoma-care nurse or your surgeon for more details. It may be that your particular operation does not involve damage to these important nerves. But if there is a possibility of such damage occurring, then you may have to adjust to changes in the sexual aspects of your relationships. I would emphasize the word 'changes'. Physical damage to important nerves does not mean that sexual aspects of your relationship have gone. It might mean that you and your partner need to develop new ways of enjoying sexual intimacy. Problems with sexual functioning can be caused by many factors other than nerve-damage. Feelings, thoughts, alcohol and some medications can have negative effects on sexual functioning. If you recognize any of the problems below, then a detailed assessment by a suitably qualified professional will identify which aspects are important for you. Discuss this with your stoma-care nurse or GP.

Some of the sexual problems which can follow stoma surgery can be helped when they are identified – especially if you think of these problems in terms of the stages of the human sexual response outlined earlier.

Reduced sex-drive

Some people who have had stoma operations notice that they lose their interest in sexual activity, that they have no desire for sex any more. Remember that you are advised to take it easy and resume sexual activities gradually – your interest may take a few weeks to return. However, if your desire for sexual activity has not returned two months after you leave hospital, then you might consider speaking to your doctor about this problem.

This problem with sexual desire can affect both men and women, and is generally associated with other changes in the relationship. A more extreme version of this problem involves a strong aversion to any sexual contact. Problems can also develop with sexual arousal, whereby men can have difficulties gaining an erection and women may experience a lack of excitement and vaginal lubrication.

Difficulty with erections

Men may notice that they have difficulty in getting an erection, or in keeping it until the completion of sexual activity. This problem is usually accompanied by a lack of sexual excitement or pleasure. You may have heard people refer to this problem as 'impotence' (or sometimes as 'erectile dysfunction'). Impotence is particularly common among men who have had a cystectomy operation (removal of the urinary bladder) with a urostomy. These problems with erections can occur following a stoma operation if the surgery has damaged the nerves which control erection. However, a man who has problems with erections does not necessarily have problems with ejaculation. This is because ejaculation and erection are controlled by different nerves within the body.

Difficulty with orgasm

Orgasm may be difficult for a man or a woman, and men may also experience problems with premature ejaculation. This means that the man will ejaculate before he wants to, or in response to hardly any stimulation at all.

Painful intercourse

Sexual intercourse can become associated with pain (called dyspareunia). This problem is more common in women, although it can occur in men. The pain usually occurs when the man inserts his penis into the vagina, or during thrusting. The pain is typically experienced near the opening of the vagina or deep inside the vagina. This sort of pain after a stoma operation is almost always due to scar tissue which has developed after surgery. It can be very distressing for the person experiencing this, and the pain can occur before, during or after intercourse. Some women develop a disorder called vaginismus – this involves recurrent or persistent spasms of the muscles on the outside of the vagina, which interfere with sexual intercourse.

Treatments generally

All of the above problems can be very distressing to the person experiencing them and to their sexual partner, especially if they'd had a fulfilling sexual relationship before the surgery. The good news is there are effective treatments for most of these problems, and that if you can tell your doctor or nurse about the problem, then they can refer you for specialist assessment and treatment. If you are troubled or worried by any of the above, you should have a further assessment. However, there may be some things which you can do in the mean time to try to help with the problem. We shall now look at some simple strategies for dealing with sexual intimacy problems such as impotence, vaginismus and pain.

The key to preventing major difficulties in any relationship is honest and open communication. Communication is an essential part of intimate relationships – you need to be able to tell your partner about your worries, how you feel, what you enjoy, etc. This may be particularly important as you both take it easy after surgery – you can tell him/her what is comfortable, what you find stimulating, what you would like him/her to do more of, etc.

Pain associated with sexual intercourse can often be helped by adopting different sexual positions. Problems with erections can also be helped if partners change there sexual positions – for example, a man who has erectile problems could try having intercourse lying on his back, with his female partner sitting astride him. There are other ways in which erections can be achieved, some of which are outlined below. Speak to your doctor if you think they may be helpful for you or your partner.

Glyceryl trinitrate patches

These patches can be stuck on to the skin of the penis. They enlarge the blood-vessels, allowing more blood to flow through the penis so that it becomes erect.

Vacuum devices

Vacuum devices consist of a cylinder which is placed over the penis; a pump then extracts air from the cylinder. This produces a partial vacuum which draws blood into the penis and produces an erection. A rubber ring is then rolled from the cylinder on to the base of the penis. This rings stops blood from leaving the penis, thus meaning that the erection can be maintained. Because the ring is in place, the cylinder can be taken off. It is also possible to obtain a condom vacuum device which does the same job, and which is worn during sexual intercourse.

Injections

The blood-flow to the penis can be increased by injecting drugs directly into the penis. Injections need to be repeated whenever an erection is required.

Implant operations

Plastic rods may be surgically inserted into the penis. These rods can be semi-rigid, to give a permanent erection, or flexible so that they can be moved when necessary. It is also possible to obtain an inflatable device whereby cylinders are implanted in the penis and a pump-mechanism is implanted in the sac. Implant surgery of this type can be complicated by problems such as infection or rejection.

If you are interested in finding out about these various ways of helping with erectile problems, speak to your GP who can refer you to a specialist in psychosexual medicine.

Lubrication

If a woman is experiencing problems with producing or maintaining an adequate amount of lubrication within the vagina, a lubricant such as KY jelly usually leads to a significant improvement. If you and your partner are using condoms because you do not wish to become pregnant, or to protect against sexually transmitted diseases, then make sure that you use a lubricant which will not damage the condom. Some of my female patients have solved this problem, increasing lubrication by using their own or their partner's saliva. This solution may not appeal to you. Remember that, as with most aspects of sexual relationships and especially intimacy after stoma surgery, almost anything goes so long as you and your partner feel comfortable with it.

'I could never speak to my doctor about sex'

After reading this chapter, you may have decided that it might be helpful to speak to your doctor or nurse about a sexual problem or another aspect of an intimate relationship. But you might be worried about this – and the worry is acting as a barrier preventing you from taking the first step. Most of us have been embarrassed at some point when having to talk about our sexual behaviour to someone else. When I see patients with sexual problems, I always explain that I understand that they might feel embarrassed or uncomfortable at first, but that I have talked to many people about intimate problems and that their embarrassment will decrease with time. Tell your doctor if you are concerned about intimacy – he or she can assess the problem, and you will soon feel at ease discussing the best ways to help.

Graded re-introduction of sexual intimacy

The general advice given above may not be enough to enable you and your partner to overcome worries and concerns about the sexual aspects of your relationship. You might want to consider trying a gradual self-help programme, to help you build intimacy back into your relationship. The gradual approach is crucial, as you may find that you have sexual urges before sexual responses have returned. One of the main causes of problems with sexual intimacy and functioning is performance-anxiety. This can be particularly difficult for someone who has had a stoma operation. Not only are they anxious about how they perform, but they are also concerned about how the stoma, the stoma appliance and their partner will 'perform'. Problems with sexual desire, sexual arousal and performance anxiety can be tackled by gradually increasing sexual intimacy. This book has emphasized that so much of living with a stoma involves taking one step at a time.

A gradual approach is especially helpful in enabling people who have had stoma surgery to regain their levels of enjoyment of sexual intimacy. To start with, you and your partner should agree that sexual intercourse is not your first aim. Your first aim is to use gentle and sensual touching as a way of beginning to feel comfortable with each other again. You should aim to touch and caress each other with your hands in a way which is enjoyable for each other. If you are touching your partner, you should try to touch parts of the body which you have not explored before. I usually recommend that the genital areas and breasts should be 'out of bounds' at this stage. This means that there is less chance of performance-anxiety or of being worried about what will happen, because you both know that your intimacy will be restricted to sensual touching and caressing. While you are being touched and caressed by your partner, try to concentrate on the sensations, relaxing and enjoying yourself, safe in the knowledge that enjoyable touching is all that will happen. As this happens, try to praise your partner when they do things that you like. You can do this in what ever way you wish – for example, by moving your partner's hand back for some more of the caressing and touching which you find most enjoyable. You can even demonstrate to your partner how you would like them to caress and touch you, and then lie back, relax and enjoy it. If you don't like your partner touching a certain part of your body, then gently move their hand elsewhere. You may notice that touching sessions make you aroused. If you feel comfortable with the idea, then you could masturbate as a response to the arousal. I usually advise couples not to move on from the gentle caressing and touching stage until they are both feeling comfortable and relaxed during such intimate moments.

As you begin to feel less anxious about these moments of intimacy, the genitals and breasts need no longer be out of bounds. You can incorporate these areas of each person's body into the caressing and touching. Remember that you should continue to give your partner feedback by guiding their hands and saying what is really pleasurable for you. In this stage of the graded intimacy programme, which includes body-parts like the penis and breasts, it is important that you do not forget to include the other body-parts during the intimate touching sessions. Some couples decide to add the use of body-lotions and massage-oils at this stage, to enhance the feelings of pleasure and intimacy. You may find that at this stage one of you becomes very aroused and may even experience an orgasm.

When you notice that the male in the partnership is getting a fairly hard erection, then the woman should invite her partner to insert his penis into her vagina. The aim of this stage is to get used to the body sensation of the penis in the vagina (this is called vaginal containment). The best position for this is with the man lying on his back and the woman kneeling above him with her knees at either side of his nipples. Try to keep the penis in the vagina for about 15 seconds – you can increase the time on each occasion if either of you is worried about going further. You should both try to concentrate on the sensations involved at this stage. Remember that the aim is to get used to each stage and be comfortable before moving on to the next stage.

By the time you are ready to begin the final stage you should be touching and being touched in a way which you enjoy, with no particular performance in mind other than enjoying yourself and giving your partner an enjoyable, intimate experience. Different couples go through this graded programme at different speeds. The speed doesn't matter so long as you move from one stage to the next when you both feel comfortable with this.

Pregnancy and contraception

Many men with a stoma have become fathers after stoma surgery. Similarly, having a stoma need not be an obstacle to a woman becoming pregnant. Many many women with a stoma have become pregnant, and given birth to many healthy babies. You may be advised to wait for a time after the stoma operation before becoming pregnant. There are various reasons for this advice. It may be to enable you to get used to looking after the stoma, or so that your abdominal muscles get a chance to strengthen. Oral contraceptive medication may not be fully effective when you have certain types of stoma, especially an ileostomy. This is because the medication may not be absorbed as it should be. In these cases you should ensure that you use other methods of contraception, such as condoms, to ensure maximum effectiveness. If you have any concerns or questions about contraception or family planning, contact a stoma-care nurse or your own doctor for further advice.

Summary

- If you are not in an intimate relationship when you have stoma surgery, it can be difficult to know if, when and how to tell someone that you have a stoma.
- If you are worried about telling someone you have a stoma, then it can be helpful to think about all your options in advance. When you have chosen an option, think about how you would deal with all possible eventualities. If you do this, you will be prepared and won't need to worry about the unexpected – you will have thought of it already. Most people find that potential partners react well to being told about the stoma.
- If you are already in a relationship, you might be worried about how your relationship will be affected. The key to dealing with this is for you and your partner to talk to one another about how you both feel about life with a stoma.
- Stoma patients are not always given information on sex and intimacy.
- The human sexual response can be divided into five stages – desire, excitement, plateau, orgasm and resolution. Problems can develop at one or more of these stages, and may be due to physical or psychological factors – or a combination of the two.
- After the stoma operation you should try to take things easy and gradually re-introduce sex and intimacy into your relationship.
- There are some simple techniques which can be used for some of the common sexual problems after surgery – such as trying different sexual positions or using a lubricant. Persistent problems can be helped by a health professional trained in psychosexual disorders.
- Many people have become pregnant after stoma surgery. Having a stoma need not be a barrier to having children.

10

Back to life

'I live a full and normal life; I eat and drink what I want, I travel, work full-time, have relationships with men and try to live life to the full' (Female ileostomy patient, aged 25).

As you become more familiar with the stoma-care appliance, begin to regain your strength, understand your emotional reactions and how your thoughts about the stoma might be influencing them, you will probably be beginning to enjoy fully some of the activities which contributed to your enjoyment of life before your stoma – activities such as eating, sleeping, travelling, working and playing sport. This chapter highlights some of the issues regarding various aspects of your quality of life in general, and aims to provide advice on how to prevent and overcome any problems or worries which may arise in these areas.

Diet

There is usually no need for a special diet following stoma surgery – unless your nurse or doctor has told you to stick to a diet because of a problem such as diabetes or high blood-pressure. In general you are advised to stick to three meals a day. However, you may find that certain foods cause you some problems, such as blockage, wind, odour, diarrhoea or a change in the colour of the waste-material. The most commonly given advice regarding eating and stoma care is to avoid certain foods if they keep causing the same problem. Remember, though, that it may be a particular brand of food which is causing you the problem – as opposed to a particular type of food. Below (page 95) is a list of foods, along with some of their most commonly associated problems – this may help you find the culprit. Do remember that everyone is different, and that some of these foods may cause you no problems at all. In the early weeks after your operation you may have a problem with a particular food – but this may be a one off incident which settles down as time goes on and as you get used to having a stoma.

If you are having a problem and you suspect that it may be due to a particular food, I suggest that you experiment on three occasions to see

94

what happens after eating it, recording your results in the Food Problem Diary below. These experiments will show whether the problem is due to a particular food. This means that you don't exclude something from your diet when it may not be the cause of the problem. You need to make sure that you leave a few days between each of your food experiments. If you get the same reaction (e.g. wind or constipation) on each occasion after eating that particular type of food, then your experiment suggests that this food is causing your particular problem.

Food Problem Diary

Type of food

Problem to be investigated

Experiment No.1   Date: _____
Result: _____

Experiment No. 2   Date: _____
Result: _____

Experiment No. 3   Date: _____
Result: _____

Have you noticed any pattern in your reaction to this food on each experiment?

....
....

After three experiments, what is your conclusion about this particular food? Remember to think about whether there are other factors which might have influenced why you had this reaction.

....
....

Does this food seem to be the main cause of this particular problem? *Yes/No*

What action will you take now as a result of these experiments? (e.g. leave this food out, do some more experiments to look for the cause, speak to my stoma-care nurse, etc.)

....

....

Food Problem Diary

Type of food

Problem to be investigated

Experiment No. 1   Date: _____
Result: _____

Experiment No. 2   Date: _____
Result: _____

Experiment No. 3   Date: _____
Result: _____

Have you noticed any pattern in your reaction to this food on each experiment?

....

....

After three experiments, what is your conclusion about this particular food? Remember to think about whether there are other factors which might have influenced why you had this reaction.

....

....

Does this food seem to be the main cause of this particular problem? *Yes/No*

What action will you take now as a result of these experiments? (e.g. leave this food out, do some more experiments to look for the cause, speak to my stoma-care nurse, etc.)

....
....

Food Problem Diary

Type of food

Problem to be investigated

Experiment No. 1   *Date:* _____
Result: _____

Experiment No. 2   *Date:* _____
Result: _____

Experiment No. 3   *Date:* _____
Result: _____

Have you noticed any pattern in your reaction to this food on each experiment?

....
....

After three experiments, what is your conclusion about this particular food? Remember to think about whether there are other factors which might have influenced why you had this reaction.

....
....

Does this food seem to be the main cause of this particular problem?   *Yes/No*

What action will you take now as a result of these experiments? (e.g. leave this food out, do some more experiments to look for the cause, speak to my stoma-care nurse, etc.)

....
....

Food Problem Diary

Type of food

Problem to be investigated

Experiment No. 1   *Date:* _____
Result: _____

Experiment No. 2   Date: _____
Result: _____

Experiment No. 3   Date: _____
Result: _____

Have you noticed any pattern in your reaction to this food on each experiment?

....

....

After three experiments, what is your conclusion about this particular food? Remember to think about whether there are other factors which might have influenced why you had this reaction.

....

....

Does this food seem to be the main cause of this particular problem? *Yes/No*

What action will you take now as a result of these experiments? (e.g. leave this food out, do some more experiments to look for the cause, speak to my stoma-care nurse, etc.)

....

....

Certain foods seem more likely to cause common problems – such as wind, odour, diarrhoea and constipation. There are no guarantees of the kind of reaction any one individual person will get – however, the next sections list some of the common culprits. If you are especially worried about your diet, then you may wish to introduce these foods gradually into your diet to see how you get on with them.

Wind ('gas' or 'flatus')

Various foods can contribute to creating wind – and some of us are born with a tendency to be more troubled with wind or gas than others. Gulping food, talking while eating, smoking, skipping meals and drinking fizzy drinks can also increase the chances of experiencing problems with wind, gas or flatus. Certain foods and drinks also increase the chances of being bothered by wind:

- alcohol
- beans
- broccoli
- Brussels sprouts
- cabbage
- cauliflower
- chewing gum
- cucumber
- fizzy drinks
- milk
- mushrooms
- nuts
- peas
- spinach
- sweetcorn
- turnip

If you suffer from wind or gas following the stoma operation, there are a number of things you can do to minimize the problem. Obviously you should do your own experiments with different foods, and avoid any which are a problem. Make sure that you chew your food well, keeping your mouth closed and waiting until you have swallowed one mouthful before you take another one. It has been suggested that drinking fennel tea, or eating two pineapple capsules (available in health food shops), or eating a very ripe banana, or eating 10–20 marshmallows, can all be effective in helping with wind problems.

Change in colour

Sometimes you may notice that the waste-material in the stoma-care appliance is a different colour. This can be alarming if you don't realize that such changes can result from eating certain foodstuffs. The following foods are particularly likely to cause a change in the colour of the waste which is collected by the stoma appliance:

- beetroot
- blueberries
- iron pills

- liquorice
- red food dye
- strawberries

If you notice a change in colour, think back to see if you have eaten any of the foods above.

Smell and odour

Some foods are associated with the production of smell and odour. If you have been bothered by an increase in the smell of your waste-material, one of the following foods may be to blame:

- asparagus
- baked beans
- broccoli
- Brussels sprouts
- cabbage
- cauliflower
- cod-liver oil
- cucumber
- eggs
- fish
- garlic
- onions
- peanut butter
- some spices
- strong cheese

If you are troubled by smells from a urostomy, you can put a spot of vinegar in the pouch to combat the odour. You should drink plenty of fluids when you have a urostomy, and try to eat foods which are high in vitamin C – this reduces the chances of your getting a urinary tract infection, and may also reduce the likelihood of smelly urine.

It has been suggested that some foods can actually reduce odour – some people claim this for peppermint oil, yoghurt and buttermilk. A soluble aspirin or some vanilla essence can be placed in a colostomy or ileostomy appliance to help prevent troublesome odours.

Diarrhoea

Diarrhoea can be caused by highly spiced foods, beans, peas, prunes, raw fruit, chocolate and spinach. It can also be caused by an increased consumption of alcohol, and can sometimes result from increased mental and physical tension. If you have an ileostomy, you should be particularly aware of the foods which have been listed as causing diarrhoea. It is also important to make sure that you drink large amounts of water, and that you have plenty of salt in your diet.

It is a good idea to tell any doctor who might be giving you medication that you have a stoma. This is because the changes to your body-functioning may mean that drugs are absorbed in different ways – this is especially important if you are being troubled by diarrhoea.

Blockages and constipation

Blockages and problems with constipation can sometimes occur. The warning-sign of a blockage is when waste-material is not produced for a longer interval than is usual for you. Sometimes the production of a watery fluid, and nothing else, is a signal that you have a blockage. As with any stoma problems which you notice or are concerned with, you should contact your doctor or stoma-care nurse for advice. If you get a blockage, don't worry too much – these are usually sorted out easily with the proper nursing or medical attention. Celery, nuts, sweetcorn and coconut are particular foods which may result in a blockage. You may need to avoid these if they keep causing you the same problem.

Sleep

Sometimes people who have had a stoma operation find that they have difficulties sleeping when they return home from hospital. This can be due to the change in environment from the hospital, and may be part of getting used to your own night-time routine and bed again. It may also be due to worries that the stoma appliance will leak during the night. Sleep-problems can be major obstacles to your return to a happy and fulfilled life after stoma surgery. Sleep has an extremely important function in restoring our energy and helping our bodies to recuperate. Getting a good sleep is therefore especially important following stoma surgery, when your body and mind are recovering from a major operation. If you have difficulty sleeping and you want to establish a good sleeping-pattern, there are a number of rules which you can follow to promote a good night's sleep.

Try to avoid heavy snacks before bed-time, and if you must have a drink it is better to choose a hot, milky drink. Alcohol and caffeinated drinks – such as coffee, cola and tea – should be avoided before bed-time. These drinks increase arousal and can disrupt your sleeping-pattern.

It may sound very basic to advise you that your bed and mattress should be comfortable and that the room temperature should be around 18°C (65°F). However, bed-comfort and room temperature are important in promoting a healthy sleeping-pattern.

Try to remember that beds are for sleeping in – they are not designed for watching TV, reading or knitting. If we do these things in bed, then our beds become linked in our minds with these activities rather than with sleeping. In other words, we start to develop the link, 'bed = TV = arousal', instead of 'bed = rest = sleep'. This means that we find it more difficult to get to sleep because we get used to being in bed when our minds and bodies are active. There are ways of getting round this problem:

- Only go to bed when you are 'sleepy tired'.
- Try to wind down towards the end of an evening. You might want to set yourself a deadline that there should be no more 'arousing' activity (physical or mental) about an hour before going to bed.
- Some people cannot get off to sleep because thoughts keep going round and round in their heads – thoughts about what they have been doing, what they will do the following day, worries about family, health, bills, etc. It often helps to write all these thoughts down on a piece of paper before you go to bed – then tell yourself that they are all there for you to pick up in the morning. There is nothing that you can do about them overnight. I sometimes use this strategy after a difficult day at work – I write down all the things which have to be done, the worries and the particular issues which need attention. Then I put this piece of paper in a drawer in my study, and tell myself that I'll collect it in the morning before I go to work.
- When you get to bed, put the light out immediately – do not read, watch TV or engage in any other 'waking' activity.
- Do not try too hard to fall asleep. You could say to yourself, 'Sleep will come when it is ready', or, 'I am rested, relaxed and calm'. If you are still awake 20 minutes later, then get up and go to sit and relax in another room. Remember that you are trying to associate bed with sleep, not tossing and turning around, reading or worrying. When you feel 'sleepy tired' again, go back to bed (wait until you do feel this even if it takes a long time – you will get into a pattern eventually). If you do not get to sleep after another 20 minutes, keep repeating this routine until you establish a regular sleep-pattern. You will develop a sleep-pattern if you stick to this programme.

- Set your alarm to go off at the same time every day.
- Make a rule not to have naps during the day, and not to sleep to catch up on lost hours of sleep.

All of these elements are essential and need to be present if you want to develop a healthy sleeping-pattern.

Travelling with a stoma

There is no reason why you cannot travel (at home or abroad) when you have a stoma. However, there are certain factors which you would be wise to take into account before you travel. It is a good idea to take at least some of your stoma-care appliances and equipment in your hand-luggage in case your luggage goes missing. Removing appliances from their boxes may give you more room in your case (though be careful not to damage them). It is also generally recommended that you estimate how much stoma-care equipment you will need – and that you then take double this quantity with you. Taking more than you need means that you'll have enough supplies to cope with more frequent changing, delays to your journey or problems with appliances which get damaged during the course of your journey. Travel insurance policies often exclude pre-existing medical conditions – and that means matters relating to a stoma. If you have a specific query relating to travel insurance, contact your stoma-care nurse, or one of the stoma patient organizations or ask your travel agent. You may be required to provide evidence in the form of a letter from your doctor about your stoma. Customs officers know what stoma appliances are. Hardly any stoma patients are ever stopped, and those who have been tell me that they have had no problems. If you are travelling abroad you will probably find it helpful to obtain a travel certificate (ask your stoma-care nurse or one of the stoma patient organizations). This outlines in different languages what a stoma involves and the steps which need to be taken to ensure that problems with missing luggage and body searches are minimized. Travel certificates usually have written information of the sort outlined below:

To whom it may concern
This is to certify that the person named on this certificate has had a surgical operation which makes it necessary for him/her to wear at all times, a bag attached to the abdomen to collect excretion from the bowel or bladder. If it is necessary to examine this bag a qualified

medical practitioner should be present because any interference may cause leakage and great discomfort and embarrassment to the wearer. The bag may be supported by a belt; if so, this may have metal parts which register on a metal detector. The owner of this certificate may also be carrying an emergency supply pack consisting of spare bags, surgical dressings, etc., in addition to his/her main luggage. It is essential that these emergency supplies remain intact and are not mislaid.

Travel certificates usually have an explanation of this type in various languages such as French, German, Spanish, Portuguese, Italian, Greek and Serbo-Croat. If you need an explanation in another language, then speak to the stoma patient associations or to your nurse. They will get this information for you. Stoma-care nurses can also give you details of how to contact a stoma-care nurse wherever you are travelling, at home or abroad.

Anyone travelling abroad needs to take sensible precautions against 'holiday tummy'. This is especially important if you have a colostomy or ileostomy – and you should make sure that you have antidiarrhoeal medication with you and that you drink only bottled water when on holiday abroad. If you have an ileostomy and you are travelling to a hot country, then you should be especially careful not to become dehydrated.

You may have concerns about staying overnight in places which are new to you. Your worries are likely to be focused on whether you have an accident and how you will deal with this. The worst-case scenario technique, described in Chapter 8, can help with these travel worries. If you are worried about leaks on bedclothes, take a special protective sheet with you. If you are worried about needing to change quickly in a strange environment, you could try to obtain a card which explains why you might need to use a toilet in a hurry, or obtain a special key for using disabled toilet facilities (see entry for RADAR in the 'Useful information' section). Your stoma-care nurse or the stoma patient organizations (addresses at the end of the book) will be able to advise you on this.

Sport

You may be concerned that engaging in physical activity – such as certain sports – could damage the stoma. It is very difficult to injure a stoma – they are very resilient and resistant to damage. In addition to this general concern, there are some sports which are associated with particular worries for stoma patients. Swimming, for example, is a particularly good form of exercise but can pose specific problems to someone with a stoma: worries that other people may notice the stoma through the swimming costume; that the appliance may fall off; embarrassment about getting changed in front of other people. Other parts of this book may help deal with these concerns (such as Chapter 6, on modifying problem-thoughts that other people may be able to detect the stoma and the appliance).

When your stoma appliance is exposed to water, the adhesive seal becomes even more secure because the adhesive properties are enhanced around water. If you don't believe this, notice that your stoma appliance is more difficult to remove in a bath. If this doesn't help you, remind yourself when you have this worry that your appliance is being held in place by your costume anyway. If, after challenging your thoughts that people can see your stoma appliance through your costume, you are still worried about this then you can wear the costume in the bath and have a look for yourself. How many people are going to be interested in what you are wearing? Do you look at the colour, shape and style of other people's costumes when you are at the swimming pool? If not, then how likely is it that other people are doing it? Next time you're at the swimming-pool, try to spot all the people with stomas. This will help you see how difficult it is. You can always buy a patterned swimming-costume and use a smaller appliance while you are swimming, if this would help you feel more comfortable, and make you less concerned that other people will notice the appliance. Some swimming-pools may have restricted times for adults or quiet times – you might feel more comfortable going at these times until your confidence returns.

There are no easy answers to worries about changing in front of other people. But there are some helpful strategies which can make this easier. You could get changed in a cubicle, or wear a long shirt when you go to the swimming-pool. Some people cope with this worry by taking a jogging suit, or something similar, to change into at the swimming-baths. They change into this when they leave the pool and then change out of their swimming costume when they get home.

If you are involved in other sporting activities, such as football or tennis, then there should be no major problems once your stoma is in place. You need to build up your fitness (just like anyone else after a major operation), and can experiment with different solutions to keep the appliance in place – such as wearing a special belt (see 'Useful information' section). If there is a risk of your stoma being hit in contact sports, you should ask your nurse about obtaining a stoma guard.

Dehydration following physical activity can be a particular problem for people with an ileostomy or a urostomy. It is important if you are involved in sporting activities to make sure that you adequately replace any fluids lost as a result of sport.

Driving

Your stoma-care nurse or doctor advises you as to when it is safe for you to drive after the stoma operation. This is usually around three or four weeks after the operation. It is not advisable to drive before this, as the physical activity involved (for example in turning the steering wheel) may cause a problem with the stoma. If you are worried about the position of a seat-belt in relation to your stoma, you can get a special device which keeps the belt off this area but still enables you to wear the belt safely. This device can be obtained from most high-street motor-accessory stores.

Work

With many of the general lifestyle issues following stoma surgery, the advice is to take things easy and work gradually towards getting back to your old lifestyle. This means that you are working slowly and steadily towards a final goal, taking small steps to boost your confidence along the way. A helpful hint for worrying, difficult or new situations is to approach them in small steps (as described in Chapter 8). Any task is easier if it is broken down into smaller, manageable chunks than if you try to deal with it all at once. Once you have conquered one part of the task, you get a sense of achievement which will not only make you feel good but also spur you on to deal with the next step in the process. If you try to go for your ultimate goal straight away, you increase the risk of being disappointed and giving up on it. You might also be less likely to try for it in the future. This is an important process to remember as you plan your return to work after the stoma operation.

Returning to work can be an important part of life with a stoma – a major step in getting back to normal. Work provides structure to your day and gives you the opportunity to test out how you are adjusting to life with your stoma. You have to deal with changing the appliance, talking to other people and doing all the things that you would usually do at work. Make sure that you don't go back to work too early, as this may cause further problems. You may not have enough energy to go back full-time straight away, or you may be worried about how you will get on. Going back part-time to start with can be very helpful for testing your stamina and coping with any worries you may have. There are some jobs which might not be suitable for someone after a stoma operation (for example, jobs involving heavy lifting). It is usually possible for an employee to discuss with their employer any problems resulting from the surgery and to come to an agreement which means that the employee can still work without risking injury. Your doctor or nurse can advise you on any aspects of your work-situation which might need to be discussed with your employer. They can also contact your employer, if you think this might help you.

Summary

- You shouldn't experience major problems with diet after stoma surgery. But certain foods can cause problems such as diarrhoea, wind and odour. Keep a note of when these problems happen, so that you can limit your intake of the foods which cause you these problems and gain control over the problem.
- Sleep is important in promoting physical and mental recovery from a stoma operation. If your sleep-pattern is disrupted, there are some things you can do to get your body back into a proper sleep-pattern. These include going to bed when you are 'sleepy tired', not reading or watching TV in bed, and dealing with worries before you get into bed.
- Travel with a stoma means being prepared – this usually involves packing appliances, finding out the name of a stoma-care nurse in case of emergencies, and getting proper insurance and a travel certificate if you are travelling abroad.
- There are no reasons why people with a stoma cannot take part in sports – the stoma does not get damaged, and most concerns you might have about sports such as swimming can be dealt with using practical coping-strategies.
- Going back to work following stoma surgery can be difficult; it is therefore best not to go back too early. It is often best to try a gradual

approach, and to speak to your employer about the stoma and continuing with your work.

Ostomy Patients' Charter

The Ostomy Patients' Charter was devised by the stoma patient organizations and the Stoma Care Nursing Forum of the Royal College of Nursing. It is printed here for your information.

The Ostomy Patients' Charter presents the special needs of this particular group of people and the care they require.

The stoma patient shall:

- *Receive pre-operative counselling to ensure that the patient is fully aware of the risks and benefits of the operation.*
- *Have a well-constructed stoma placed at an appropriate site, having regard to the comfort of the patient.*
- *Receive experienced stoma nursing in the post-operative period.*
- *Receive full and impartial information about all relevant supplies and products available through the NHS.*
- *Have the opportunity to choose from a wide variety of products without prejudice.*
- *Receive experienced stoma nursing and medical support in both the hospital and the community.*
- *Be given information about the three National Stoma Associations and the advice, counselling and support they provide.*
- *Receive support through information to family, carers and friends to increase understanding of the condition and the ability to adjust to the stoma.*

Useful information

Stoma patient organizations

The three stoma patient organizations provide patients with information and support before and after surgery. These organizations often have local contacts who can provide you with information on what they do and what support they might be able to provide.

British Colostomy Association
15 Station Road
Reading
Berkshire RG1 1LG
Helpline: 01734 391537

Urostomy Association (Central Office)
'Buckland'
Beaumont Park
Danbury
Essex CM3 4DE
Telephone and fax: 01245 224294

ia (The Ileostomy Association and Internal Pouch Support Group)
Amblehurst House
PO Box 23
Mansfield
Notts NG18 4TT
Telephone: 01623 28099

Appliance manufacturers

I have included the names and addresses of some of the main appliance manufacturers. Most of them have Freephone telephone numbers with trained nursing staff to advise on appliances and stoma care.

Dansac Ltd
Victory House
Vision Park
Histon
Cambridge CB4 4ZR
Freephone: 0800 581117

ConvaTec Ltd
Freepost
Harrington House
Milton Road
Ickenham
Middlesex UB10 8BR
Freephone: 0800 282254

Salt & Son
Lord Street
Birmingham B7 4DS
Freephone: 0800 626388

Coloplast Ltd
Peterborough Business Park
Peterborough
Cambs PE2 6FX
Freephone: 0800 220622

SIMS Portex Ltd
1–3 High Street
Hythe
Kent CT21 5AB
Telephone: 01303 260551

CliniMed Ltd
Cavell House
Knaves Beech Way
Loudwater
High Wycombe
Bucks HP10 9QY
Freephone: 0800 585125

Pelican Healthcare Ltd
Cardiff Business Park
Cardiff CF4 5WF
Freephone: 0800 318282

Marlen (UK) Ltd
Unit F4C
Keighley Business Centre
South Street
Keighley BD21 1AG
Freephone: 0800 317602

Welland Medical Ltd
6/7 Brunel Centre
Newton Road
Crawley
West Sussex RH10 2TU
Freephone: 0800 136213

Hollister Ltd
Rectory Court
42 Broad Street
Wokingham
Berkshire RG40 1AB
Telephone: 0118 989 5000

Other useful contacts

Amcare
Freephone: 0800 88 50 50

This company provides an ostomy appliance ordering and delivery service.

RADAR
12 City Forum
250 City Road
London EC1 8AF

This organization runs a scheme for better access to public lavatories. They provide details enabling you to access special toilet facilities by purchasing a key from them.

SASH
Woodhouse
Woodside Road
Hockley
Essex SS5 4RU
Telephone: 01702 206502

This company produces a stoma hernia belt. It is available on NHS prescription and may be helpful to protect the stoma, and keep appliances securely in place.

BACUP
Helping People Living with Cancer
3 Bath Place
Rivington Street
London EC2A 3JR
Cancer Information Service – Freephone: 0800 18 11 99
Cancer Counselling Service – Telephone: 0171 696 9000 or 0141 553 1553

This national charity gives information, counselling and support to people with cancer, their families and friends. Information booklets are available on cancer and cancer treatments.

Magazines for stoma patients
Various magazines are produced for people with a stoma. These can be obtained by contacting the magazines directly.

Talkabout	*Freephone*: 0800 525350
Spectrum	*Freephone*: 0800 282254
Your Choice	Freepost NG 1317, Newark NG24 3YZ

Resources for nurses and surgeons

Surgeons and nurses who are interested in obtaining copies of monitoring materials used in this book (e.g. Appliance Confidence Monitoring Form, Trials Monitoring Form, Food Problem Diary, etc.) to promote adjustment to stoma surgery should contact Dr C.A. White, CCPS, Strathdoon House, 50 Racecourse Road, Ayr KA7 2UZ.

Further reading

Greenberger, D. and Padesky, C.A., *Mind Over Mood. A Cognitive Therapy Manual for Clients*. The Guildford Press, 1995.

Mullen, B.D. and McGinn, K.A., *The Ostomy Book. Living Comfortably With Colostomies, Ileostomies and Urostomies*. Bull Publishing Company, 1992.

Northover, J.M.A. and Kettner, J.D., *Bowel Cancer: The Facts*. Oxford University Press, 1992.

Index